SKETCHES FROM VIETNAM

Jonathan Cape · Thirty Bedford Square London

SKETCHES FROM VIETNAM

Written by RICHARD WEST

Illustrated by

GERALD SCARFE

FIRST PUBLISHED IN 1968
© 1966, 1967, 1968 BY RICHARD WEST
ILLUSTRATIONS © 1966, 1967, 1968, BY GERALD SCARFE
JONATHAN CAPE LTD, 30 BEDFORD SQUARE, LONDON, W.C.I

SBN 224 61345 6

PRINTED IN GREAT BRITAIN BY
EBENEZER BAYLIS AND SON LTD
THE TRINITY PRESS, WORCESTER, AND LONDON
ON PAPER MADE BY JOHN DICKINSON AND CO. LTD
BOUND BY A. W. BAIN AND CO. LTD, LONDON

CONTENTS

LIST OF ILLUSTRATIONS

INTRODUCTION

I WROTE THIS BOOK AFTER THREE VISITS TO SOUTH VIETNAM IN 1966 and 1967. I went the first time out of curiosity and the next two times because I had grown fond of the country. Although I went there at my own expense, I wrote a number of newspaper articles in order to help meet the cost. Certain passages of this book have appeared in the *Listener*, the *New Statesman*, the *Daily Mail*, the *Sydney Morning Herald*, the *New York Times Magazine* and *Private Eye*.

This is not a book about the war. While travelling round the country I sometimes lodged with operational units and occasionally witnessed the war. But most of the fighting takes place in jungles and mountains far from the towns and paddy fields where the mass of the people live. Of course the war sometimes intrudes into 'safe' towns like Saigon and Dalat, as it did very violently early this year. But ordinary life is soon resumed.

The book begins, returns to, and ends in Saigon. The rest is divided among the three great geographical regions of South Vietnam: the northernmost provinces close to the border with North Vietnam; the Highlands, where the tribesmen live; and the rich heavily peopled Mekong Delta. Most of the travel was done by air, as the roads and railways are usually 'insecure'. I am grateful to countless pilots of the U.S. Army, Navy, Air Force, Marines and above all the C.I.A. (who control the Air America company) for their readiness to give lifts and their skill in flying.

This is not a book about politics. Everybody now knows the arguments for and against American intervention in Vietnam. In describing what I observed in Vietnam I have tried as far as is possible to exclude my own view about who is to blame for the tragedy.

Gerald Scarfe's drawings speak for themselves. The Vietnamese, who are witty and quick, were enthralled by his caricatures of themselves. The Americans, on the whole, were not. The French proprietor of a restaurant who had asked Scarfe to paint a mural was so appalled by one quick sketch of himself that he burned the dinner.

1968   R.W.

Chapter One SAIGON

THE REGAL HOTEL IS ONLY A HUNDRED YARDS FROM THE CENTRE OF
Saigon but few foreigners stay there or have heard of it. Before the
Second World War the Regal was patronized by minor French officials
and their families who had come from up country to shop and hear the
gossip. A notice under the glass on the reception desk says: 'The Regal
Hotel is a homely hotel'—and therefore does not allow guests to bring
in women. It is one of the few hotels in Saigon that still enforces the
rule.

Some guests in the past have shied away from the Regal because they
have seen rats in the lobby and, worse, these were black rats such as
spread the plague that is rampant in Vietnam. If you complain about
the rats to the men at the reception desk, they laugh and shrug their
shoulders, knowing only too well that rats roam freely these days in
Saigon and that traps are useless to keep them away. The nearer you
get to the river, the more rats you see; and even at one of the grand
hotels a foreign woman, returning from up country, discovered a nest
of baby rats beneath her pillow. Rats have been seen in the penthouse
restaurant of the grandest hotel of all.

The cockroaches are fewer than in New York and you seldom find
more than one in any one room. The Vietnamese, who are so ready to
kill each other, think it is bad luck to kill cockroaches. They remember
the poor student of fairy story who spared the life of a cockroach
which later revealed itself as the Buddha and guided the student's hand
in the big exam. And the Vietnamese are taught from earliest childhood never to touch the lizards on the wall. The lizards of Vietnam
are coloured like fresh putty and looked to me more squat and plump
than those in the rest of the East. They seldom utter the characteristic
harsh *tack tack* but instead creep about in silent and ceaseless strategic
movements—with undiscernible motives of hunting or murder or
lust. Bats complete the wild life of the hotel. If you leave your window

open at night they fly in and soon become hypnotized by the turning fan in the ceiling. They follow the blades round and round until they get tired and sweep giddily down over the furniture. People here say that the bats are rabid so it is best to get rid of them quick by switching the light and the fan off and letting the creatures find their way out of the window. Swallows nest under the eaves of the houses, and there used to be many pigeons. However, the street urchins last February used a ladder to get to the top of the pollard trees and rob the pigeons' nests. The parent birds wheeled overhead in distress as the boys took the ladder from tree to tree in the avenue. A crowd, of course, gathered to watch; perhaps they thought that one of the climbers might fall off the tree and into the rush-hour traffic below.

The Regal proprietor, Mr Oscar, is French, but he has lived for forty years in Indo-China, and even before that he served with the army in Senegal ('quand j'ai fait l'Afrique') and in Syria. Sometimes, in moments of melancholy, he will recall the great moon of Aleppo that rises over the central avenue in a giant, silver hemisphere; but he seldom speaks of France. The memory of the homeland that he has not seen for forty-five years is either too poignant or too remote for words. Mr Oscar's face is creased with a thousand lines like the physical map of some mountainous country. When he winks, to bring home the joke of some anecdote, both eyes close tight like asterisks. The war, the previous war, the Second World War, the various foreign invasions and all the shocks and ironies of his life in Indo-China have given Mr Oscar a deep and comforting scepticism. He has seen it all and accepts nothing. But in his relationship with his friends he is courteous, always considerate and always interested in the latest jokes and gossip. He is friendly towards us English and he often talks about Graham Greene who was here in Saigon during the fifties. But the memory of the author has somehow become confused with his memory of *The Quiet American*, which Greene wrote while he was here. Of course Monsieur Greene was right to have the American killed; the man had been ill-mannered enough to steal Greene's girl from under his eyes. By the way, Mr Oscar asked, did Greene ever take that girl back to England with him?

Mr Oscar's list of personnel includes boys, 'boyesses' and even two coolies to help in the kitchen, but there is nothing colonial or feudal about the character of his staff. They are friendly, inquisitive, honest and quite free from servility. The reception desk clerks, the room boys and the bar waiters take an immediate interest in the name and occupation of each new guest. 'Everybody here knows you are English, not American,' Mr Oscar said on my third day. 'Not just the people in the hotel, but everyone for several blocks around. They're very intelligent people, the Vietnamese, and they love to gossip.' Within hours of my checking in, the hotel staff had examined and criticized my clothes, hair style, and even the Soviet wristwatch I carry. One of the older bar waiters, named Dan, extended a welcome in what I later recognized as his own sardonic style. 'You are lucky to be in this hotel, Monsieur. It's not expensive and it's safe. One day, not very far from now, the Caravelle will go *bham!*' Here he jerked his arm upwards and leered like an evil Chinaman on the movies, with eyes narrowed to slits of mischief. 'Continental Hotel, *bham!* Last week a bomb went off in a restaurant and seven Americans were killed.' At this he burst into a fit of giggles. On this very first day, Dan regaled me with one of his strange and oracular statements about the political situation in Vietnam. Either because his French was inadequate, or because his real views were too heterodox for expression, his message came out obscure. 'Vietnam!' he explained with one of his Chinese-villain smiles, and a secretive glance round the room. 'First we had the Japanese ... *ech!* Then the French ... *ech!* Now the Americans ... *ech!* The big fish eats the small fish and the small fish eats the smaller fish still. *Grong poissong monge p'tit poissong. Petit poissong monge poissong plus p'tit!*' Having said this, he closed his eyes into slits again and uttered a sinister chuckle.

The narrow, L-shaped bar is reminiscent of France. The back wall is filled with dusty and empty bottles of Ricard, Vermouth, Byrrh and Black Rum. The gramophone records include French songs such as Edith Piaf's, light classics, and mournful Vietnamese melodies for the sake of the staff. Two young, very beautiful and reserved girls take turns at the cash register. They spend most of the time sorting through batches of photographs of themselves or studying English out of a book. They disdain to practise their English by talking with customers, whom they despise. There are also a few other girls employed as hostesses for the Americans. They drink tea with them, listen to them or maybe only pretend to listen to them. They are said to be fairly chaste.

One small, wizened waiter named Nam has worked here for more than twenty-five years. He is a very cheerful, dignified man who seems to take great delight in what he is doing—whether eating a sandwich or puffing a cigarette. He is very quiet and reserved except when a pedlar or shoe-shine boy enters the bar. If Nam does not approve of this particular pedlar, he flies at him, screaming abuse, exactly like a scottie dog getting rid of a stray cat from the drawing-room. Whatever he shouts seems to make its effect, because the intruders retreat in great haste long before Nam has even so much as come round the bar. After these outbreaks, Nam looks round the company with a gratified smile just to show he is not really as fierce as he makes out.

On my first day in Saigon an incident took place in this bar. An American customer, who was drunker than all the rest, suddenly yelled at the waiter who served him a gin and tonic: 'I said vodka, you fucking fool!' The waiter poured out a vodka and tonic and then placed a metal spoon in the glass in order to stir the ice. It is the French custom, and reckoned good form in Vietnam. 'Get the fucking hardware out of here!' yelled the American, and hurled the spoon across the bar. 'You haven't got the manners of a bastard duck,' he added, for good measure. This was a bad mistake. Foreigners often compare the high-pitched, quacking sound of the Vietnamese language to 'copulating ducks'. The Vietnamese think it an insult to mimic another man's voice and they hate the degrading comparison. It was the duck remark that provoked the trouble this day. The pretty cashier and the barmaids were already enraged against the American. Their bosoms heaved with angry gasps and their eyes had opened unnaturally wide like the dragon ladies of folklore. Suddenly one of the girls ran round to the front of the bar and hurled herself on the American. 'Don't you come here and shit the Vietnamese people! Shit the American people! Get out of here!' she yelled; then, losing her grip on the English language, she picked up the glass of vodka and tonic and hurled it away.

This American, like most of his fellow-countrymen whom one meets in Saigon and the other cities, was not a soldier but one of the great tribe of civilians. About five thousand are engineers under contract to the U.S. Government for construction work. There are many other sales representatives, auto dealers, sellers of unit trust shares and maintenance men. To these one should add some of the junior ranks of diplomatic and A.I.D. clerks, technical experts, petty spies and mechanics. The government employees try their best to behave with proper decorum in front of the Vietnamese. No inhibitions of this kind affect the engineers and the other purely mercenary U.S. civilians.

Early one morning the Regal Hotel awoke to the roar of a newly arrived construction engineer. 'You drunken son of a bitch,' he was yelling at one of the servants. 'Pull this out, you dumb son of a bitch.' I found him sitting on the stairs—a tall, spectacled man, like a brainless Arthur Miller—who had checked out a few days before but still expected to find a room ready for him. It was nine o'clock, always the time of his drunken rage, for by mid-morning he lapsed into maudlin incoherence. He stumbled into the hotel lobby and buttonholed Scarfe and myself. 'I just told this man out here that America rules the world. You know that's true, don't you?' he added in wheedling fashion. 'I like you, Ted [he always addressed me as Ted]. I'd buy you anything. But America rules the fucking world.' He kept on repeating this favourite cry to the lobby, the bar and the street outside.

These Americans hate the British and French who come to the bar. One morning an English colleague and I were discussing *The Quiet American* and how much Saigon had changed since Graham Greene was here. From the other end of the room we heard a Mid-Western voice say 'phoney limeys'. After a pause the speaker repeated: 'I wanna hear from them phoney limeys what they think of the Americans.' We went over to meet the speaker, a mean-mouthed, rat-eyed fellow of forty-five or so, with a greying crew-cut. He claimed that my friend had used the expression 'lousy Americans'. We denied this. 'Lousy' is not a word that the English use. 'All right,' he persisted, 'you said something derogatory about the Americans.'

'We were talking about a book called *The Quiet American.*'

'So you're trying to imply that I'm a loud American? Is that it?'

He is loud, but not much louder than most of his chums. They broadcast their problems and grudges and miseries to the world. 'I'm going to Hong Kong and I'm going to fix me a divorce. Then I'm going to Los Angeles and I'm going to commit mass murder—my wife, my two exes and two son-of-a-bitch attorneys ... Have you ever seen a Chinese fall down two floors of an open elevator shaft? It happened in my hotel last night. Really funny. Mind you, it was his fault. This American fellow couldn't get the elevator door open so he had this argument and just picked this man up and threw him down ... Do you remember Joe? He threw a man out of a third-floor window—that's second-floor as you reckon it [he explained for the benefit of the limey]. This fellow had been put in the same room. Joe had never met him before. He just came in that night and picked him up by the neck and the seat of the ass and threw him out of the window. This fellow was in hospital three months. Luckily for him he fell flat on his stomach on the sloping roof below then slid down into the street. If he'd gone straight down he'd have broken his neck and his back.'

More than four thousand Americans are employed by R.M.K.-B.R.J. —a consortium of American companies that handles 75 per cent of U.S. construction work in South Vietnam. It spends more than one million dollars a day on airstrips, docks, roads and communication systems. The American employees earn an average of 1,100 dollars a month plus a 275-dollar cost-of-living allowance as well as a free return air fare. Many are chronic wanderers round the military bases and oil fields of America overseas. Most are in their thirties, forties and fifties. When R.M.K.-B.R.J. began operating in Vietnam in 1962, it could not be too choosy about the type of man employed. 'Half a man is better than no man when you've got to build something by yesterday,' I was told by James A. Lilly, the general manager in Saigon. 'Now', he said in a warning voice, 'the marginals are going to be surplused.' Many were 'surplused' during the following month. There was even a sign at the headquarters of R.M.K.-B.R.J. that said: 'Spitting on the floor will be cause for immediate termination.'

These very neurotic civilians suffer most from sexual frustration. Their term of employment in Vietnam is eighteen months, or six months more than the soldiers. The U.S. Government tries to prevent any American from bringing his wife and family to the country because of the shortage of lodgings and schools and also because of the hypothetical danger. Nineteen out of twenty civilian contractors have agreed in their contract to leave their families in the United States. Moreover, they have to spend five hundred and ten days of their eighteen-month tour away from the United States so as to qualify for relief from income tax. A few have managed to smuggle over their wives. A few have found Vietnamese mistresses, especially middle-aged widows. The majority have to make do with prostitutes. Ordinary Vietnamese girls do not care for the engineers; they talk too loudly, drink too much, belch, and commit various breaches of Vietnamese etiquette. As a result, most of the engineers are lonely and given to self-

18

pity. Their tough-guy talk is sugared with sentimentality; their hairy chests are bedewed with salt tears.

One lugubrious engineer who drinks in the Regal Hotel remembers always the happy days in Korea. He knows a few words of Korean and tries these out on the bar staff. He gets angry when they do not understand, although Korean is quite unlike Vietnamese. 'If you go into a bar in Korea—a man like you or me of forty or forty-five—' he told a buddy one day, 'and you meet a girl there, she's probably aged about twenty. And she wants to learn everything you know. She wants to learn from all those years of experience of yours. She becomes like a servant to you. There's love and devotion such as you've never experienced.' A younger salesman complained to me: 'I've only met three girls here who had hearts of gold, and two of them were peasants. I met an ugly American broad once. She was thirty-three and past her prime but it was so lovely to lie in bed there beside her in the dark and talk and understand what she was saying that I thought she was the Queen of Sheba ... Besides, she enjoyed screwing.'

One man who had been airing his detestation of Negroes became all of a sudden woebegone as he told of a certain friend who 'regularly takes groups of Vietnamese children to visit the ice-cream parlour for a treat. One day he left the key in the car and asked a Vietnamese to fetch it for him. But the Vietnamese somehow turned the key which in a Chevrolet starts the car, which in consequence ran into a group of people killing a pregnant woman. He was only trying to help—to be nice to the Vietnamese. But you can't do a damned thing right here.'

These civilians love to talk or just to soliloquize. One man, a former civilian pilot in the Congo, talks of the job that his wife once had in a brassière factory. 'Boy,' he recalls over and over again, 'you saw some of the biggest tits there you ever saw in your life.' The Vietnamese girls, who are proud of their finely proportioned bosoms, detest this man. His friend is an Ethiopian whose job I never discovered. 'I am the oldest Jew in the world,' he says. 'I'm the only one, the lion of Judah. I'll fight anyone who takes the land of Judah. Do you know what's going to happen in Ethiopia? Nothing's going to happen. Do you know what Haile Selassie said to Nasser? "All the genius comes from Jews." Einstein, Oppenheimer ... ' at which the pilot interrupted: 'Oppenheimer, Schloppenheimer, you Judah bastard!' and both of them fell silent and glum. An elderly pianist called Charlie Bourne, who entertains at the Officers' Club, approached me and asked: 'Could you do me a favour? Just write a column beginning "I was a stranger in town. I had no experience, my own experience that is. And then I met a little piano player called Charlie Bourne. And from then on I began to understand." ' If I was an atheist, said Mr Bourne, then nobody would publish what I wrote. 'I'm the greatest Christian Scientist you ever met. I wouldn't be surprised if I was the only Christian Scientist over here.' Many of these civilians appear to be unemployed. I asked one of them how he got along without a job. He grinned in a knowing way. 'They say I'm unemployed. I pretend I'm broke. Do you believe that? I've been here many years. I speak Vietnamese. Do you imagine I'd be broke? Do you imagine I'd be doing the job I pretend?' A great many Americans in Vietnam are employed by the C.I.A. Those who are pretend they are not. Those who are not often pretend they are.

These civilians are very warlike towards the Vietcong, the North Vietnamese and the Chinese. Indeed they are much more belligerent than the troops themselves. 'Some of these guys,' said a contemptuous soldier, 'who've never carried a gun before in their lives, are going around with a forty-five like they was in *Gunsmoke*.' I have seen civilians pouring bursts from a Thompson machine gun into some rice fields they said were V.C. territory. Another one told me how he had watched a napalm strike on the enemy and he said it 'was really a lot of fun.' One plump, Pickwickian man in the Regal Hotel wants an immediate nuclear hit against China to bring her eight hundred million people to death by starvation. He calls himself a 'hawk' but he looks like a fascist potato, and that is the name we give him. 'I think we should keep turning the heat on,' he says, 'but just like they've got their Buddhists here, we've got our Buddhists back in Washington. Walter Lippmann's the chief. I'd just like to get my hands on that man.'

The troops out in the country are very much more likeable. These civilians provoked an unfair remark in my diary: 'Saigon used to be called the Pearl of the Orient. The pearl has been cast before swine.'

* * *

One of the many illusions held about Vietnam by people who have not been there is that Saigon is remote from the war or 'behind the lines'.

In fact there are no real 'lines' in Vietnam; and Saigon itself is an area of the most intense and regular fighting. Even in the centre of the town, where the main hotels are situated, one can hear the sound of bombing at most times of day. At night one is frequently woken up by the noise of bombs, artillery and machine-gun fire. Flares often illuminate the city. A Vietnamese friend who lives in one of the outer suburbs says that he often loses nights of sleep as American aeroplanes bomb within a few hundred yards of his home. There are many places in Vietnam where you could spend a month without hearing a shot or a bomb; in Saigon the war bangs continually in the eardrums.

Yet, and this is another puzzling paradox, Saigon is very safe. When reading about the last days of the French, you are struck by the atmosphere of terror and jumpiness. In those days one could not sit at an outside café for fear of grenades or the more dreaded land-mines. The Vietminh, precursors of the Vietcong, employed assassination and terror as instruments of the liberation war. Scarcely a day went by without the murder of some European. All that has now changed. The Vietcong have brought off a few deeds of terrorism: against an American officer's quarters near my hotel, a dingy floating restaurant on the Saigon River, and even the U.S. Embassy. But these incidents are as isolated and rare as were *plastique* attacks in Paris during the last days of the war in Algeria. There are no guards on the bars where Americans visit, no districts of town where Europeans are not allowed, no mention of danger in everyday conversation. In Aden, during the anti-British terrorism, I have felt nervous walking at night; and indeed there were daily bombings and shooting aimed expressly at British people. In Saigon I never felt a moment's fear. It may be that the Vietcong, in contrast to the Vietminh, do not believe in terror as a political instrument. It may be that the Vietnamese police have a good system of counter-intelligence. In colonial days—just as in British Aden—the job of detecting terrorists was left to foreign policemen who did not know the local language and customs. Terrorism today is less easy.

From all accounts Saigon is much nastier now, although fairly safe, than it was in French colonial times when grenades were thrown into restaurants. It is, for example, grossly overcrowded. Hundreds of thousands of refugees have moved in from the countryside to escape from the Vietcong (as Americans say) or American bombing (as others say). It has all the signs of a cramped city; there are shanty-towns,

unpaved streets, piles of rubble and building work with all its con-
comitant dust, noise and ugliness. Much of the building goes on quick-
return projects like luxury flats and night-clubs; the characteristic
sight of new Saigon is a half-finished night-club surrounded by rusty
barbed wire. The convoys of old American trucks have added their
black diesel smoke to the impure fumes of the bastard petrol used by
the Vietnamese in their motorbikes and auto-cycles. At evening, when
the mist hangs heavy and hot in the city, the reek of this rancid gasoline
makes you gag and gasp for sweet air. Rubbish collection is sometimes
slow in these affluent times; but fortunately the Vietnamese, unlike
some Asians, are clean by habit and do not defecate in the street.

Many visitors have expressed their horror and shock at the blatant
black-marketeering in Saigon. You can buy almost every item of U.S.
Forces goods, from a pair of combat boots to a tinned Christmas
pudding. This display annoys the Americans much more than it does
the neutral outsider. Americans feel, with understandable rage, that
the Vietnamese are making a quick profit out of the war. In particular
they become incensed by rumours that American guns and ammunition
change hands on the black market. Moreover, much of the merchandise is false. The bottles of spirits are drained and refilled with local
hooch. The transistor sets and watches are often faulty. The street
hawkers who offer you two hundred and fifty piastres a dollar are quick-
change confidence tricksters who try to palm off counterfeit notes.

The heat seems hotter in Saigon than elsewhere although, while I
was there, the thermometer never went higher than ninety-five
degrees. The Vietnamese complain of the heat as much as the Europeans
do. It is blamed for their bouts of laziness, for their melancholy, for
their colds and their stomach trouble and above all for 'spring fever'.
The symptoms of 'spring fever', which lasts the year round, are inability to sleep at night or to come right awake by day. Another symp-
tom is loss of appetite. Because the Vietnamese cannot face a big meal
they eat snacks throughout the day, mostly of ham sandwiches, rice
and fish sauce, nuts and oranges. The street vendors also provide more
potent dishes for jaded Saigon appetites. Roast sparrow, ram's testicles,
frogs, snakes and hot dogs (made from real dog) are popular. My
favourite lunch was curried eel, a small bowl of rice and yoghurt. The
French restaurants have gone into decline since the Americans came
but they too follow the Saigon fashion for strong tastes like heavily

peppered *steak au poivre*, pungent garlic sausages, onion soup packed solid with cheese, and goat's cheese laced with raw onion. Vietnamese anglers say that provincial fish will take simple baits such as worms and crickets but Saigon fish have to be tempted by bits of steak or cheese paste.

The people, as well as their appetites, are jaded. In the exhaustion of making money to pay for the ever-increasing bills, the Saigonese have no time or will to relax. There are few cafés or dance halls for the Vietnamese themselves—the entertainers have learned English and gone to play for the G.I.s. There is no regular ballet or theatre in the Vietnamese style. One Sunday afternoon I went to the race-course at Phu Tho, on the other side of Cholon, which before the Second World War, Mr Oscar informed me, was almost as elegant as Longchamps. There were Arab and European horses, and he himself had once owned a fine chestnut which had, unfortunately, been poisoned by enemies on the eve of the big race. The track today is tawdry and sad. The yellow and red cement grandstands have started to crumble in tropic fashion. The track which is more than a mile round is edged on the other side by factories. The scrubland inside the track has grown so dense that a regiment of Vietcong could take shelter there without the spectators knowing the difference. Swarms of dragon-flies blunder around the paddock, looking like miniatures of the helicopters that chatter their way over the course. When I saw the jockeys weighing in, I thought that there must be a change of programme and that these were participants in a children's gymkhana. The average jockey, in boots and holding his saddle, weighed in at about thirty kilos. The largest tipped the scale at thirty-five kilos and cannot himself have weighed more than four stone. These tiny boys are said to be fifteen years old but they look no older than six. However, it turned out that the horses themselves, who were led in soon by the grooms, were several hands shorter than any English racehorse. They were rangy, bad-tempered creatures that kicked the spectators whenever they got the chance. The horseshoes, piled by one of the stables, could fit quite easily into a man's palm. The starting point for each race was on the other side of the course and as these ponies were led across I wondered how many would have the energy left to race back to the finishing point. It proved to have been an accurate speculation. By the end of the race, the entire field had slowed down to a kind of half-canter. The

23

SAIGON BAR

69355

baby jockeys whipped their horses across the head and even, in fury, whipped each other. Three were disqualified in the first race. The patrons in the reserved stands were big Chinese wearing shark-skin suits, ties and hats. They had the serene look of all rich Chinese as they drew on their black-market American cigars and sipped their adulterated whisky.

You see many children's games being played on the streets of Saigon but normally it is grown-ups who play them. There is pitch-and-toss and an elaborate version of noughts-and-crosses involving forty or more squares. The old men are particularly good at this game. Sometimes you see little girls playing hopscotch but most children in Saigon are too busy earning a living to bother with childish things. It is one of the curious and distressing results of the war that anyone under the age of eighteen in a Vietnamese city is likely to earn twice as much as his father. The bootblacks are 'number one' in American Forces slang. They can earn ten piastres a shine from the Vietnamese but the Americans often pay them as much as fifty piastres. A hard-working shoe-shine boy with a good pitch in a popular café is likely to earn as much as a pound a day, which is very good money by Vietnamese standards. Of course they importune people for custom; they wheedle and start to polish your shoes before you can turn them away. But they are far less irritating than shoe-shine boys in other parts of the world. The Vietnamese pride or diffidence puts a restraint on even the most impudent pimp. If one answers one of these children with a polite refusal—by pointing out for example that suède shoes do not need a shine—he will remember your face and greet you next day with a courteous smile.

The same goes for the news vendors. They deal in the English-language newspapers—the *Saigon Daily News* and the *Saigon Post*—as well as magazines like *Time* and *Newsweek*. The dailies sell at the high price of fifteen piastres a copy so that the boys probably earn almost threepence a copy. These boys too are persistent salesmen. If you are not holding a newspaper, they beg you to buy one. If you *are* holding a newspaper, and can be presumed to have read it, they ask you to give the newspaper back to be refolded and resold. Vietnam must be the only country in the world where you can open your morning newspaper and find that someone else has already solved the crossword puzzle. 'You buy paper, Mister? You give me paper, Mister?'

Many children are simply criminals. The most innocuous of these offer to guard your parked car—and punch a hole through the tyre if you will not accept. One American told me he paid out about a pound a week in protection money but he did not mind, for the children sometimes polished the paint and always prevented other children from breaking in. About two hundred thousand children in South Vietnam are officially classified by the government as juvenile delinquents. Most are wallet-snatchers and watch-thieves. There is one little girl whose head scarcely reaches my knee who sells packets of cough drops or edible seeds. At first glance she is sweet, or 'cute', as they say in America. Then you notice the shifty look in her eyes and her whore's manner of rubbing against your leg. I thought of the Dostoevski villain who dreamed of a small girl and saw her face transformed into that of a leering whore. The tiny cough-drop girl is the decoy for a boy thief. While you talk to her and try to brush her away, the boy sidles up and grabs your fountain pen or your camera. Children, so I was told, also serve as messengers for the many gambling syndicates and dope rings.

They say that twenty years ago there was no juvenile crime in Vietnam because of the family discipline and the reverence for parents. The commotion of the war has broken up many families. There are seventy-seven orphanages in South Vietnam but a survey last year showed that three-quarters of all the occupants had one or both parents living. Some poor refugees despair of trying to feed all the children and give the youngest into the care of the state. Handicapped children— regarded by Vietnamese as bringers of bad luck—are also frequently sent to orphanages. The American troops, who are lonely and starved of affection, smother these orphans and pseudo-orphans with money and gifts. 'Their over-generosity doesn't always help,' said Richard Evans, an American adviser to the Minister of Social Affairs. He had met the same problem during the war in Korea when soldiers would make a pet of some particular orphan. 'One little kid of five had his own little uniform with sergeant's stripes, hand-made combat boots, two lockers (one of them filled with candy), a private room with a folding bed and his tailored uniforms on a clothes-rack. Nice deal! At every damned orphanage in this country you can see American servicemen giving money or surplus food to the kids.'

Thousands of Americans both in Vietnam and the United States want to adopt Vietnamese children. This wish is no doubt prompted by pity for children seen on television; there may also be a feeling of guilt because American bombing has helped to create orphans. However, the South Vietnamese Government is very unwilling to let children leave the country and it has banned the adoption abroad of all but a few children. Many Americans help a Vietnamese child through an organization called Foster-Parents Plan. They make a monthly payment towards a needy Vietnamese family; and the child, in return, writes a monthly letter of thanks. These letters, translated by Vietnamese, have a curious, old-fashioned tone: 'There have been two serious fires in my area recently ... The noise of children singing loudly is coming through my window ... My siblings are all fine.'

A Roman Catholic priest named Ho Dac Khan runs what he calls a 'doss-house for shoe-shine boys' in Cholon. He got the idea a few years ago when a boy offered to shine his shoes. 'I could tell by the way he spoke that he was well brought up,' said Father Khan, with a typical Vietnamese reverence for the 'good family'. 'I asked him why he did this work and he said because of his granny. Many of these boys are of good family but they get led astray by the promise of fortunes in Saigon. So they steal some money and then they're ashamed to go back to the family.' Father Khan was bitter about the treatment given these boys by the Saigon police. 'Sometimes the police leave them alone for days. Then they are told that they have to fill up the van with prisoners so they pick up all the boys they see and take them off to prison for three days. Afterwards the boys come to me in tears and say: "But Father, I didn't do anything wrong." '

The street children of Saigon look almost too hard for tears; it is one of the childish things, like playing, for which they have lost the capability. The toughest of all end in one of the state penitentiaries, such as Thu Duc, north of Saigon. Our guide, Mr Evans, said that an element of the boys were just 'damned little Dillingers. There's nothing you can do about them until they get old enough to go to prison.' One of the first boys I met was only eight years old, and serving a sentence for pickpocketing. He stood stiffly to attention and regarded me with the shifty eyes and tight smile of an old lag. His gums and mouth were a mass of rotting, white infection and his voice had a hoarse, wheedling tone. He looked very, very old. Two of the boys here were sentenced for murder. One of them had killed his best friend with a kick in the genitals. Another, of thirteen, had a tattoo on his arm saying: 'I hate the girl who has betrayed me.'

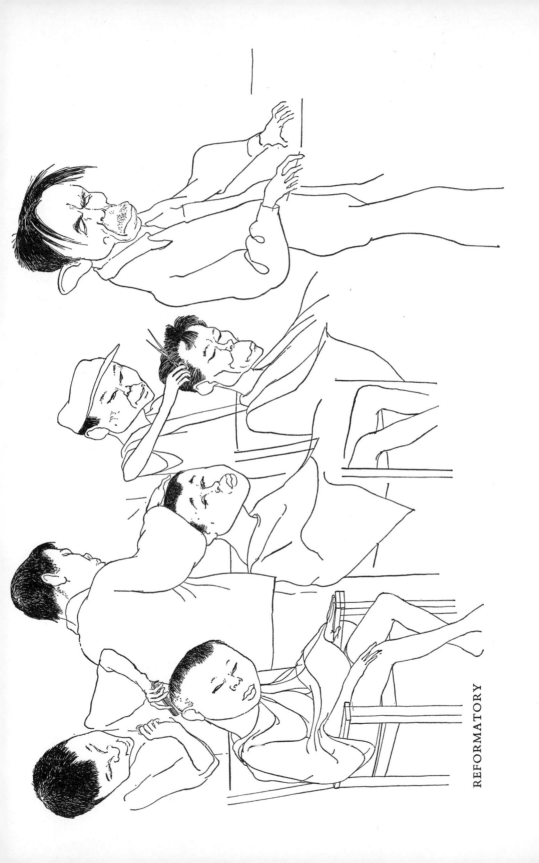

REFORMATORY

The boys at Thu Duc are encouraged to learn trades such as black-smithing, weaving, carpentry and hairdressing. But they know very well that crime, in Vietnam's war economy, will pay much better than any of these. The warders too, who are ill paid and even worse trained, bring no sense of enthusiasm to the work of reformation. The children spend their pocket money on cigarettes and they smoke quite openly in front of the staff, although, by the rule-book, smoking is not allowed. All these children were born and grew up in a time of war and at twenty-three they will have to join the army. Until that time they are war profiteers.

Early last year the boys' prison enjoyed its formal opening. As Mr Evans described it: 'We had a corner-stone laying and the Prime Minister came along. He flew his own helicopter on to the meadow out there. We had a hell of a job trying to get the children to sing for him. They couldn't get into key. They just weren't interested.'

* * *

Whenever Saigon got depressing I went to the zoo on the other side of the Prime Minister's office. The lawns are well watered and tended; the trees and shrubs grow tall as befits a botanical garden; the museums and the pagoda on either side of the entrance gate are newly painted and cheerful. The Saigonese appreciate these things and the zoo is widely patronized. On Mondays the animals do not need to be fed because of the masses of peanuts and bamboo shoots they are given over the week-ends. Even on weekdays you normally have to queue for your ticket. Since few Americans go there, foreigners are made welcome. A group of girls ask you to take their photograph; a boy asks you to hold him up to fetch a kite from a tree; the children who clutch your hand are not for once trying to pick your pocket. Lovers walk there or go for a row on the river. The far side is filled with troops of boy scouts who practise their knots or fieldcraft or camp-fire cooking.

Even the zoo has had its grey moments. The Japanese put an ammunition dump here and Diem used part of it as a prison. Although several ex-prisoners now say they were held under the tigers' cage, they were in fact in the offices of the director. Even there, at night, the roar of the tigers must have been loud. The tigers are still an object of terror to many Vietnamese, who say that they have the evil eye. Visitors to the zoo prefer the lions, which come from Africa via Japan. I have heard it said in Saigon that 'the lioness makes love like a woman, lying on her back. They gnaw at each other, of course, but otherwise it is just like a man and a woman.' Maybe this odd belief explains the continual crowd by the lions' cage. People are almost as interested in gorillas, which the Vietnamese compare, in jest, to Americans, saying that both species have long arms and hair all over the body. The snake house is popular during feeding-time when the keepers put live ducks in the cage. The ducks sit in a corner, side by side, with a look of extreme unhappiness, while the pythons doze and work up an appetite. The impatient boys in the crowd throw small stones at the cage to try and wake up the snakes or panic the ducks into waking them.

The zoo director, Vu Ngoc Tan, explained that most of the animals came from South Vietnam. The most valuable of the imports were the zebra, the chimpanzee and the monkey-eating eagle from the Philippines. He is very proud of the chimpanzee 'which is not so tame as yours in London. It likes to chew children's finger. I prefer them like that. We are not in the circus business here.' Moreover, just as in other zoos, the humans are guilty of violence to the animals. One of the Saigon gorillas died after eating a bun stuffed with ground glass, and some children stoned a crocodile to death.

The elephants here are tame commercial animals that move about their cage in a ceaseless soft-shoe shuffle. There used to be herds of elephants round Saigon, Mr Tan said, but now the remaining few were up in the Highlands near Cambodia. War had made animals dear as well as scarce because the tigers that used to come from Tay Ninh were now getting sold to American soldiers. But Mr Tan is determined to build up the national wild life. Deer from the zoo are taken to Phu Quoc island and dogs from the island are sold to the international market. Even such drab beasts as the hog deer and the spotted deer could earn their keep on the market, he said. 'They are very resistant to disease and we give them to underdeveloped people instead of cattle. Also the horns are very popular in oriental medicine and if we cut them off they may sell for three times the price of the deer.'

Few tourists in Saigon visit the zoo. The inquisitive and the seekers after excitement normally ask first of all for a look at the monks, whom they have seen at prayer or committing suicide on television. Of course only a few monks set fire to themselves or take part in street demonstrations. There are quietists and contemplatives such as the 'coconut monk' from My Tho who sat in a tree for nineteen years ignoring the Vietminh and the Vietcong, the French and the Americans. Many monks and Buddhist laymen condemn the savagery of the extremists, while imploring foreigners from the West 'not to judge us by them'. Buddhists from other countries, too, are shocked by some of their brothers in Vietnam. A Thai girl whom I knew in Saigon never ceased to be shocked by them. 'They're very bad men. They like to fight together although Buddha says they shouldn't. And they're very rich. Do you know that I once saw a monk with a girl outside a night-club? Champion!' The foreign journalists, just as censorious, have to pass many hours at the An Quang pagoda, which looks more like a run-down school than the main holy place of the Buddhists and headquarters of their main political movement. The walls are peeling and decked with rusty barbed wire. The courtyard is dusty on dry days and flooded on wet days so that you have to cross on stepping stones.

Even in the pagoda proper the children ask you for cigarettes, hit you, make faces and pluck at the hair on your arms. There are always a few surly and slovenly men in boy scout uniform. They do not respond to the boy scout salute or any other scout lore. Their very appearance would take years off the life of an English scoutmaster. However they do have the useful job of driving the children away with blows of a rolled-up newspaper.

There are many monks with shaven heads and robes of orange, yellow or white. Those with office jobs work at typewriters, ledgers and telephones. The majority loaf about smoking, grinning and simpering. There are also a number of journalists hanging about in the hope of getting a photograph of a monk burning himself to death. More persistent journalists ask for interviews with one of the Buddhist leaders, but the monks always answer with one of the few phrases they know in English and French: 'No understand,' 'I forget,' and 'Come back at eight.' When you come back at eight they say: 'Come back at eight tomorrow.' This obtuse attitude maddens the foreign newspapermen. 'All I want to know, Venerable,' said one persistent correspondent, 'is whether we can expect a self-immolation this evening. You see we have a deadline to catch.' Then, turning to one of his colleagues, he muttered: 'Goddam it! How on earth am I going to explain "deadline"?'

32

DA NANG, WHICH THE FRENCH CALLED TOURANE, IS THE second city in South Vietnam and the most northerly port. The Vietcong and their helpers from North Vietnam are strong in this district which Vietnamese call the Centre and the French called Annam. It is close to the borders of North Vietnam and the jungles of Laos which serve the Vietcong as a base and a means of escape. It is also a district of militant Buddhists and politicians hostile to Saigon. There were bad riots in Da Nang in the spring of 1966 and, in consequence, all public places were put off limits to U.S. servicemen. It is the base for the Marine Corps in Vietnam and a major port for shipping. The oil from the freighters and tankers has made the bay too dirty for swimming, but Vietnamese fishermen still paddle their boats and cast their nets among the rusty hulls of the foreign vessels. Da Nang is also a great air base. An American boasted to me that they had built here the first parallel jet runway in all Asia. The Vietcong often attack this air base with mortars or rockets and they sometimes machine-gun planes at landing and take-off. Three U.S. planes crashed during the first three days I spent in Da Nang and several helicopters were smashed by grenade fire.

It is a dirty, sullen city. The prodigious military building programme has churned up much of the waterfront and cast its dust over the villas and parks and avenues of the residential district. Barbed wire and blocks of cement serve as barriers for these building projects and scores of sentries watch over the barriers. But since the American soldiers are friendly, sociable people they allow the Vietnamese to wander almost at will among the military installations. Old women squat next to cases of ammunition piled on the dock; youths lean against the naval headquarters; children, many of Vietcong age, cluster round the sentry boxes to cadge cigarettes, peer at the sentries' comic books and practise their scraps of English. (At forward units in battle zones, I noticed peasants grazing their cattle among the artillery and even beside a general's tent.)

The limitation on U.S. troops has had a distressing effect on the Da Nang economy. The shoe-shine boys know the meaning of slump. The cyclo (or pedicab) drivers almost beg for your custom. Instead of bringing their prices down to attract business, they stake all on finding just one colossal sucker. The cyclo-man who had taken me three hundred yards asked for five hundred piastres (nearly two pounds). I offered him five piastres; he settled with great pleasure for fifty. The many bars and hamburger restaurants that started in 1964 to serve the Marines now have to make do with customers from the Merchant Navy. The bar girls have learned to say 'Smooth sailings' as well as the usual 'Sorry about that! No kidding!' The Chinese proprietor of the same bar complained that while quite recently he had lived *comme il faut* on two thousand piastres a month, he now needed six thousand a month because of the rising costs. He blamed the war and the Americans for having made the rich richer and the poor poorer. To make matters worse, the Americans no longer came to his bar because of the ban.

Even in Da Nang there were moments of beauty. I saw a Vietnamese girl of about fifteen—in trailing *ao dai* dress and pantaloons and conical hat—who had rashly begun to walk across a freshly tarred road. After a couple of footsteps, one of her plastic sandals stuck. She had to stop to extract the shoe and as she stopped the other also got caught. At every slow step across the road she looked more vexed and more desperate, like a white butterfly caught in a pool of jam. Then, just as she was nearly across, she chanced to look up and see me watching her progress. Her rosebud mouth which had been pursed up with worry suddenly split in a smile; she leaned back, took off her conical hat, brushed the back of her hand against her forehead and said in a nasal, plaintive and altogether enchanting voice: 'Number ten'—which is Japanese and American and now Vietnamese for 'bad'.

Some mutual friends had asked us to call on a lady who shall be known as Madame Da Nang. The title Madame comes to mind because of the famous Madame Nhu who virtually ruled South Vietnam in the early 'sixties. Many Vietnamese ladies of beauty and elegance have an uncomfortable likeness to Madame Nhu. Our Madame Da Nang, for example, came from the same district of Hué. She was also of very good family, and liked to remind you of it. She had just returned from Mass when we called the first time and she was wearing a dark blue *ao dai* in the quiet, almost sombre style of the centre and north. Her opening questions, I later learned, were standard in high society. 'How old are you?' — then 'How old am I?' Here she simpered and rubbed her hands with a rinsing motion. 'I am fifty,' she said and started giggling again. Now although it is hard for foreigners to guess at the age of the Vietnamese, we knew that her sister was twenty-four, and Madame Da Nang looked about thirty. Her face was lined but only beneath the right eye, as though from some nervous tic or special exhaustion. When we had revealed our ages, Madame Da Nang said that all Vietnamese people now looked older than their years because they were very unhappy. 'I am very poor,' she added, and then started to rinse her hands and simper again. 'I am very poor,' she repeated, 'and when my cousin goes to Switzerland this winter I shall ask her to buy me diamonds there because they are cheaper than here. In Saigon they are very expensive.' It turned out that Madame Da Nang was not in the least poor. She owned a number of restaurants and a cinema and had let her villa to the Americans at a big rent. 'If I was not so poor,' she said, 'I would build a big cinema.'

Madame Da Nang's house is built in the usual Vietnamese fashion. The entrance off the street is shabby and humble but gives way to a lavish front room, which leads on to less elegant bedrooms, then to the kitchen and bathroom, and finally to the servants' quarters out in the back yard. It is like a Victorian London house built on a horizontal instead of a vertical plane.

In Madame Da Nang's house I tasted my first and best Vietnamese meals: crab soup, meat noodle soup, fried fish, thin slices of pounded and spiced steak, meat balls, stewed duck, a little rice, followed by lotos fruit stuffed with nuts. The flavour is more delicate than the Chinese food that we get in England; it is also distinguished by the notorious, ill-smelling *nuoc mam* or fish sauce into which one dips every mouthful of food. The Vietnamese observe the excellent Chinese custom that all the guests leave as soon as the meal is over.

The meal is no more than a rite at the end of the entertainment. It is meant to follow rather than fuel the conversation and wit. Most of Madame Da Nang's conversation was centred on the Americans. She did not like France, where her husband was, or, by association, Europe. The country she liked best was Japan and she had learned Japanese during their occupation. But although she had been to Japan it did not gratify her romantic imagination. America, above all Hawaii and California, was really the place she wanted to live, because 'American women do not have to work and are very pretty.' When she said this I understood the significance of the strange picture that hung in the corner behind her chair. It was an oil painting, eight feet high, of the film actress Sandra Dee. One of Miss Dee's films had been showing at Madame Da Nang's cinema. She 'saw Sandra Dee and how beautiful she was and asked a Chinese artist to make the portrait'. The final result was astonishing. The huge pouting lips, the blank, bulging eyes, and eyelashes as big as quill pens lowered with colossal cuteness over the room. On the other side of the door there was another work by the Chinese painter which I thought I recognized as a portrait of Brigitte Bardot. I complimented Madame Da Nang on having acquired such a good likeness. Fortunately she did not understand what I said for the woman who looked like Bardot was really Madame Da Nang's young sister as seen through the artist's imagination. All Madame Da Nang's decorations showed the same taste. There were cheap nude statuettes of nymphs and playgirls, ornamental bottles of whisky, souvenir ashtrays from Texas and Honolulu, bottles of scent and glossy American magazines. Madame Da Nang had fallen in love with the West just as many Americans fall in love with the East. Her decorations and tastes were Chinoiserie in reverse. Just as an English girl, at the turn of the century, might have been painted with pigtails and slanted eyes and a dashing kimono, so Madame Da Nang's younger sister appeared with a pert pout and round, saucy eyes.

In spite of these affectations, Madame Da Nang is thoroughly Vietnamese. 'For some time people of good family would not let a Vietnamese woman marry an American. Then one girl went to the United States and she was very happy. So now we think differently.' However she did not really want to leave Vietnam for more than a few weeks and she disapproved of Americans who made their girl friends pregnant and then went home. Even Vietnamese men were wicked these days, she went on. They were much too fond of *choy boy*. We looked puzzled and Madame Da Nang repeated *choy boy*. After a few moments of giggles and hand-wringing she got out her English-Vietnamese dictionary and read out the translation of *choy boy*—'to lead a debauched life'.

*　　*　　*

The provinces round Da Nang were occupied hundreds of years ago by the Tiams, a people similar to the present Cambodians. Later the Vietnamese drove the Tiams not only from Annam, the centre of Vietnam, but from Cochin China, the delta region in the south which includes Saigon. They massacred the Tiams, expropriated their paddy fields and their irrigation canals, and neglected their beautiful temples. The French recovered many Tiam works of art and established a small museum for them at Da Nang. It was shut after the Buddhist riots in 1966 and the grounds were enclosed by rolls of barbed wire. The space in front is used by the U.S. military as an embarkation site and is normally cluttered with yellow construction machinery, stacks of ammunition, and companies of newly arrived troops. However, in 1967 a force of Marines were set to work on restoring this little museum as part of their 'Civic Action' programme and they allowed me to take a look round. There were many busts of Tiam kings, always portrayed with a fierce, mocking expression, many lions, elephants and wriggling dancing girls such as you see at Angkor Wat in Cambodia. These are works of an Indian culture that is alien to the Vietnamese, whose ancestors came from China. The French creation of Indo-China tried to combine the people of Indian culture—the Cambodians and the Laotians—with the more aggressive, more numerous people of Chinese culture—the Vietnamese. The two elements never fused and they still distrust each other. The North Vietnamese have invaded Laos, and once fought the Cambodians. The leaders of South Vietnam would dearly like to invade Cambodia once they have settled accounts with the Communists. The Vietnamese, as the world knows only too well, are a warlike and obstinate people. Yet when I mentioned the Tiams to a certain girl in Saigon she grew mournful and even ashamed. 'That's why we're suffering now,' she said, 'because of the Tiams. When we massacred them we condemned ourselves to generations of war. All Vietnamese believe in the curse of the Tiams and if you haven't heard about it before it's only because you're a foreigner.'

The ancient empire of the Tiams in the area round Da Nang is now ruled by the U.S. Marine Corps. These legendary troops, nicknamed 'leathernecks', who have battled their way, in the words of the song, 'from the halls of Montezuma to the shores of Trip-o-lee', are responsible for the whole I Corps territory, which is the northern quarter of South Vietnam. Since landing in 1965, the Marines have pushed the

Communist forces out of the valleys and into the mountainous jungles of the interior where the war is fierce and horrible. The Communists have an easy line of supply to North Vietnam and indeed many regular units from up north have come to join in the fighting. But since the mass of the population lives in the coastal plains it is controlled by the government. This does not mean that the people like the government. Even most Americans will admit that about half the population in I Corps are active or passive supporters of the Communists. The Marines are determined to change this and they therefore give much time and energy to befriending the locals or 'winning the hearts and minds of the people'. I spent a week with Marines in Quang Nam province, south-west of Da Nang, to observe this 'pacification', this 'other war'.

One instrument of 'pacification' is the County Fair—an attractive name with echoes of Morris dancing and Dan Archer—which is both a civic and a military action. I attended two of these fairs near Hill 55, a batallion headquarters in a strongly contested area twenty miles south of Da Nang. A lieutenant explained the principle of the fair: at midnight a company of Marines would surround the neighbouring village, preventing all movement of people in and out. At first light a company of ARVIN, the South Vietnamese Army, would sweep through the village arresting known or suspected Vietcong, searching out tunnels and other hide-outs, and forcing any armed enemy to make a dash through the cordon of waiting Marines. Meanwhile the villagers would be led to a neighbouring camp where they would see some of the benefits of loyalty to the Saigon government.

I got on the first of four lorries bringing the ARVIN soldiers next morning. A tank and a mine-clearer went on ahead—more than twenty Marines had been killed or wounded by mines in the previous week— and our progress was so slow that dawn had broken before we reached the village half a mile away. The ARVIN soldiers smoked and giggled and no doubt hoped that the foreign fool would fall off the back of the lorry. One of them was masturbating. We got off the lorry and walked to the village. The Marine corporal in front of me—who insisted that we walked fifteen yards apart—took great care not to tread on the young lettuce plants in the furrow, and moved with a strange, splay-legged gait. The village, like most in Vietnam, is scattered about in clumps of trees. Each cottage is half hidden by shrubs and wide banana leaves. 'This is a real poor village,' said a Marine sergeant. 'Their

39

SOLDIER IN BARRACK HUT

shelters are no good. No head covering.' Even the smallest hut in this part of Vietnam has its family shelter against the bombs and howitzer shrapnel.

At 7.24 an ARVIN officer told the villagers over the loud-speaker to pack their valuables and prepare to leave, but there was no immediate sign of movement. 'These people don't want to go no place,' the sergeant said. 'It's always the same story.' Then he reported down the field telephone: 'It's going a little slow. They're eating chow right now.' We walked to the north-west edge of the village that looked over a paddy field to a line of trees about six hundred yards away. The corporal said in a philosophical tone of voice: 'We've found a lot of women and children but no men. Yet somebody's got to make the babies.' A burst of automatic fire came from the trees. I joined two Marines who were taking cover behind a bank. One, a Negro, was reading a paperback. His white comrade was keeping his head down and laughing. They had two more days left in Vietnam and were 'demob happy', as English soldiers say.

The ARVIN soldiers started their search, at the end of which they would in turn be searched by their own officers to make sure they had not stolen a fowl or some household valuables. In any case, the villagers took no chances. The women lugged away everything on their shoulders or in baskets slung from poles: children, pigs, cooking utensils, bedding, rice and vegetables. They moved barefoot in single file down the earth dikes through the paddy fields, silent and sullen themselves, but laden with squalling children and squawking ducks. When the villagers were gone, the ARVIN soldiers prodded the ground with bamboo poles and discovered a V.C. hide-out tucked in the edge of a garden. The entrance was not so wide as a foxhole but two V.C. could hide in this lair. The snipers from across the paddy field kept up a desultory fire as ARVIN blew up the tunnel with dynamite.

By half past nine the two-hundred women, old men and children were camped in tents by the main road about four hundred yards from their village. The Marines conducted a census helped by an ARVIN officer and a bad-tempered man who had once been a V.C. The Marine officers referred to him as a defector; the Marine other-ranks as a turncoat. Medical orderlies treated the villagers for their skin ailments, cuts and minor shrapnel wounds; they distributed handfuls of chewable vitamins. The villagers queued up in apparent delight to have their bad teeth pulled by a dentist. The other Americans chatted and dozed and made their meal of C rations washed down with Funny Face Drink Mix.

The Marines are helped in these county fairs by an eager and brash Army lieutenant who recently came to Vietnam as a graduate of the John F. Kennedy School of Psychological Warfare at Fort Bragg. His absolute certitude and his air of innocence brought to mind Lieutenant Dub and Cadet Biegler from Hašek's *The Good Soldier Schweik*. The lieutenant parroted every cliché of modern psywar: 'The Vietcong can only keep their support through fear ... The only way they can keep the people believing is by isolating them. As soon as the people hear something else they believe it. The minute you begin speaking to someone you make him stop and think ... Just meeting these people is something. A smile can do wonders. We're saying to them: "We're here to stay and we want you to know it. If you attempt to challenge us, we'll flatten you like a bug ... But we're prepared to forgive." '

The psywar lieutenant had failed in his principal task of bringing Vietnamese music to entertain the villagers. The Marines therefore played a tape recording that one of the men had just been sent by his mother; it proved to be of Bob Dylan protest songs. The Americans and the Vietnamese listened in equal boredom to yowling denunciations of war in Vietnam and mournful thoughts 'on the eve of destruction'. At noon a few sniper rounds pinged overhead and ARVIN blew up another tunnel.

By the afternoon most of the village children were chewing gum or puffing cigarettes. Sometimes they made a raid on the garbage can and got driven off by Marines. A medical orderly said that seventy-five per cent of the local children he treated had cuts on the feet from stepping on tins in military rubbish heaps. The psywar lieutenant put on a Walt Disney film about hygiene; but it was too hot in the darkened tent. The dentist gave a demonstration of how mothers should wash a baby. He soaped and splashed and towelled the bewildered little boy while one of the officers gave a commentary through the interpreter. 'Tell them not to let the baby scratch,' he announced, then added in an aside: 'Goddam it, if I had a rash like that between my legs I'd cut my balls off.' When the first little boy was washed another started to take off his clothes but the Marines wanted the mother to wash him. She refused, cursed, tipped the water out of the basin and stalked off in a huff. Only a few of the village women had come to watch the washing.

By 3.30 the heat was fierce but the Marines persuaded a few children to take part in a sack race. There were Hershey Bars and Tropical Bars and Bit-o-Honey for every child who finished the course. They even persuaded the old men—with packets of fags as prizes—to join in a three-legged race that caused much merriment to the Americans, who crowded round the finishing post with their cameras.

A county fair normally lasts for at least two days while the villagers sleep under canvas. But tempers are short by the end. The women fight for their handouts of mouthwash and rice. The cripples brandish their crutches like clubs. The children steal. The V.C. defector whined to the Marines that they should not pass on Band-aids to the villagers who would only pass them on to the V.C. Later he hit a child in the back with a well-flung and full Coca-Cola tin. 'Number ten,' said an angry Marine; 'that's number ten public relations.' But this county fair had at least proved a minor success. The officer in charge said they had caught two V.C.esses or women Vietcong: 'They were sort of prostitute age and we think they were banging for the V.C. … We know one of them is a cadre but we don't know which one.' In the end they let them both go. The psywar lieutenant, his big blue eyes gleaming with self-satisfaction, said that 'this war is like trying to grab smoke. When you open your fist there's nothing there.' Such is the wisdom taught at the John F. Kennedy School of Psychological Warfare at Fort Bragg.

* * *

Critics of the American role in South Vietnam say that the military fight the war at long range—and above all by aeroplane—rather than by staying among the peasants. The Marines alone have to live in some of the villages seized from the Vietcong, and this experiment is an interesting feature of 'pacification'. I visited two Marine Combined Action Companies, known to the men as CACs. Both teams were commanded by sergeants. Both lived in villages that had been captured during the last year. Both worked with units of Popular Force who are local auxiliaries employed on a part-time basis.

'We live with the people but not like the people,' a young corporal explained to me at Hoc Phu. 'We keep our standards high so that the Popular Force have something to strive up to.' Although, out of politeness, the Marines sometimes accept village meals of rice, pork and duck, they prefer their C rations of tinned steak, ham and crackers. They live in their own compound guarded by barbed wire, bunkers, and claymore mines that can blast buckshot for hundreds of yards. 'Social life is just about nil,' said the same corporal, 'and I don't reckon to walk into Da Nang more than once a month.'

This CAC team is led by Sergeant C. P. Soape, an exuberant chap from Dallas, Texas. 'All but one man in this team', he said, 'has volunteered for another six months in Vietnam. And as for that one man, I'm working on him too.' He claimed that the Vietcong no longer dared to attack, and when they had come to the village for rice a few weeks ago they came unarmed and were sent away. Last year was the first rice harvest without a tax to the V.C. 'We're part of the community and we get just enough combat to make it interesting. I don't think we're doing a great deal but if you change anything in the Orient you're doing a lot.'

There are sixty-eight CACs in this northern quarter of South Vietnam where the Marines operate. Most journalists and officials are taken to Hoc Phu. 'We get a lot of visitors here,' said Sergeant Soape as a Uruguayan reporter appeared in a Jeep. A few minutes later a great roaring wind swept over the paddy fields as a helicopter descended, all gleaming grasshopper green. A famous journalist had arrived with a man in a black tie. 'C.I.A.,' the Marines said. The man in the black tie approached a sergeant, asked for his pistol, and tucked it into his belt. He then strode off to the village. 'Does that damned fool come here often?' the sergeant asked. 'Two or three times a week,' the Marine replied. In twenty minutes the famous journalist and the man in the black tie were ready to take off again. The journalist had his story and the man in the black tie had jammed the pistol.

Even Sergeant Soape does not pretend that all is well in the village. As soon as the Vietcong had been pushed out, the Catholic Church claimed a tax on the dam it owns in the neighbourhood. 'The Church takes three out of ten baskets of rice,' the sergeant said, 'but that dam was built when the French were here and these peasants probably built it. They're so regimented that if you tell them they owe you fifteen dollars, they pay. That's the discouraging thing. We run out the bad guys and another lot of bad guys come in.' He cheered up when we went to call on a favourite local citizen who had built a new house from U.S.A.I.D.* bricks. 'Give a little bow to that altar,' said Sergeant Soape. 'It's just about all he's got. He's built that for his son so he'll have a good time in the next life. Life's so bad in Vietnam that by the time they're fifteen they're starting to plan for the next life. They've been so shot to hell in this.'

The success of a CAC team must depend on its Popular Force allies. One Marine captain told me that many Popular Forces did a deal with the Communists in a village and warned them when the Marines were coming to do a search. He also accused them of torturing Vietcong prisoners. Village girls, he said, who flirted with the Marines were savagely beaten and even expelled by the Popular Force. But in Hoc Phu, which is overwhelmingly Catholic and therefore inclined to be anti-Communist, most of the Popular Force have proved their loyalty to the Marines and have even risked heavy fire to defend them. It was Popular Force pay-day when I arrived and I saw them cycling back from town with their purchases. One man had a hundred-pound bag of corn, donated to Vietnam by the people of the United States, which he had just bought for twelve shillings on the black market. Another, wearing four hand grenades, two bandoliers, a carbine and a combat knife, had just bought a child's cap pistol. He banged off round after round in a cloud of cordite.

Later I saw a CAC team near Dai Loc where there had been heavy fighting a few months before. 'A lot of the people were killed by the V.C.' the sergeant said, 'and a lot by us. We've made a lot of friends out here. At first they were frightened because the V.C. said we were going to kill their buffaloes and rape their wives … But we're the good guys now, so they're with us. That's the Asian way.' The sergeant was rather amused by his new job as administrator and do-gooder. 'I was in Korea when I was eighteen years old and then you didn't see any civilians. Anything that moved you shot.'

The Marines in Vietnam are far removed from the grisly, brutal fellows of World War II and the Hollywood epics. They are intel-lectually superior to their counterparts in the infantry or indeed in the British Army. The officers have studied the problem of Vietnam and read even the critical books. Many Marine other-ranks have college degrees or are planning to go to college. A number have learned the difficult Vietnamese language. The old-style braggarts and chest-

* United States Agency for International Development.

46

beaters are mostly the older men who re-entered the Corps from retirement. 'They wrote and asked me to re-enlist,' said one of these, 'and I did it for Corps and Country. And because I was mad at the draft-card burners and Vietnik bastards who are against everything.' His was a voice from the past. The new Marines must study to be gentle and this sometimes produces a certain neurosis. The sergeants and warrant officers in my barrack hut were confirmed sleep-talkers. The man who sat up most of the night obsessively cleaning his pistol would say in his dreams that 'it's all very complicated.' Even the crackshot sniper in the corner would shout in his sleep 'I can't do it.' By day he was full of reasoned advice on his trade: 'At one hundred yards you aim at the crotch and hit the chest cavity. At three hundred yards you aim at the head and hit the chest cavity.' Battle fatigue may explain some of these bad nerves but so too may the strain on a lion obliged to lie down with the lamb.

Nobody should imagine that CAC teams, or similar Civic Action by fighting men, can quickly 'win the hearts and minds of the people'. The peasants of Vietnam have seen too many invaders to be impressed. The Japanese were the most popular. The French used Civic Action teams identical to the CACs. The Vietcong, whatever Americans care to think, do not get their way by terror alone. However, CACs have certain distinct advantages. Their presence guarantees the villagers against further American bombing. They make it difficult for the Vietcong to operate and raise food. They provide a permanent evidence of the government's power. Moreover, to do the Marines justice, they are quite kindly and well-mannered troops. Unlike the ARVIN, they seldom rape or steal. The main fault of the CAC system is simply one of scale. To make it operate in all the disputed hamlets of South Vietnam would require, I should estimate, at least three million American troops compared with the present five hundred thousand.

*   *   *

Lieutenant-Colonel W. R. Corson, commander of the 3rd Marine Tank Battalion near Da Nang, and later appointed commander of all the CAC teams, has an individual attitude to the eleven thousand Vietnamese in his district. He wants them to make money. 'The Bible tells you that the rich man doesn't get into heaven because it's so damned painful. Well I'd like to raise that threshold of pain. Maybe the Lord loves the generous giver but the recipient doesn't ... We're going to build a pig-pen here and when it's finished I want to see a twenty-two-inch dollar sign bolted over the door.' This eccentric but very remarkable soldier-scholar has known Vietnam for fifteen years and has strong theories about the problem of 'pacification' — 'that's the vogue word at present, isn't it?'

Most Americans try to obtain the confidence of the Vietnamese by gifts of food or toys or by MEDCAP field medical clinics. Colonel Corson despises 'charity in any form' and says that 'MEDCAP is just handing out goodies.' He won the respect of the village of Phong Bac by teaching Marines to play Elephant Chess, known in China as Bao Chi and in Vietnam as Co Thuong. 'With this you can establish a crowd all over the Orient. They all think it's their national game and they all take a pride in their prowess. Our Marines play it well enough to beat them and so now it appears that we're not dilettantes. We're very good at something that is important to them. We organized a tournament and each hamlet put forward its champions. On the night of the harvest moon we held the play-off and presented a prize of a fifty-five dollar radio. This showed that we were taking more than a passing interest. This changed us from being the Big Nose and the Running Devil.'

Colonel Corson spent more than twenty years in the Far East with various agencies before returning to Vietnam and his present combat duties. He speaks several Chinese dialects and understands Vietnamese. He claims that he can beat the Vietnamese at Bao Chi thanks to the tips he acquires from reading the Bao Chi page in the Hong Kong Communist newspaper. He is also writing a history of the Imperial Chinese monetary system and this gives a clue to his favourite passion of economics. Adam Smith is his hero; but he has read them all and will quote even Marxists to prove his point about South Vietnam. 'There's misery in being exploited. There's even greater misery in not being exploited.' In the spare time from his main job of running a tank battalion, Colonel Corson thinks out ways to exploit his local village.

Rice is the main crop but is too involved with politics. 'The French stuck this country with monoculture and the soil has been badly leeched. The land round here is owned by the Chinese in Da Nang and rents run at about fifty per cent. Then there's government tax. Then the Catholic Church wants to take thirty per cent. The attitude of the bloody priests is: "We're glad the Americans have come so that we can get our due." So you may find that out of his crop the peasant is only left with twenty per cent.' Colonel Corson looked about for other ways to 'spring the profit motive on these people'. He thought of fishing in the river and taught his Marines to bomb the water with obsolescent grenades. Soon the fishermen were netting immense, concussed fish which were sold at a fair price on the local market. The money went to a village fund. 'Now we're on the verge of going into the pig business in a big way,' Colonel Corson explained. He has also begun a lumber and an apiary business. 'Bees will literally work themselves to death for you. Yet nobody in U.S.A.I.D. knew about bees. But I read an article in the *Wall Street Journal* (I have an airmail subscription) about how to keep bees and we're going to make mead. A friend of mine who's a director of Sears Roebuck said: "We could almost replace sacramental wine if we could get Phong Bac mead."'

The U.S.A.I.D. authorities in Vietnam will normally set up a village committee to thrash out problems of credits, improvements and grants. Colonel Corson has set up a business committee. His aim is that the villagers should decide who is most capable of exploiting new business ventures. 'These people know who's got the ability. The A.I.D. people don't know. It's a cruel selection process—to the best goes more.' The Vietcong are active in Phong Bac and recently shot a Marine through the head. Colonel Corson challenged them to debate with him on an evening during the Christmas truce in the confident belief that 'my theoretical dialectics are much better than any that came out of the Novotny Institute in Moscow.' The V.C. refused the invitation but they did hold their own Christmas meeting at which they said that 'all the Americans want to do is to turn you into a bunch of money grubbers.' The Colonel was delighted. 'Do you know that bit in *The Brothers Karamazov* when Dostoevsky says: "Scratch a peasant and you get a petty bourgeois"? Well, I'm scratching like mad! I'd sure as hell prefer a petty bourgeois any day to a peasant.'

Colonel Corson has no use for the 'fucking altruists' in the U.S. Embassy and the A.I.D. mission. 'I don't give a damn about the Vietnamese peasant any more than I do about the bloody Welsh miner on the dole. I care about the interests of the United States. That's why you're here. You're here to sell newspapers and if anybody says you care about the bloody wogs they're talking —' The colonel smiled at his own wicked talk and then took off on a discourse about the Enclosure Acts, William the Conqueror, Imperial Vietnamese history and theories of marginal profitability. Colonel Corson says he has 'no Messianic complex. I don't give a rat's rear end what happens in other units but here we're having a lot of fun. That may not be the right attitude in time of war but you've got to do something to pass the time. That's the Third Tank Battalion for you.'

Of course Colonel Corson really cares for the peasants of Phong Bac. His bitterness is that of the military man—the 'man in the field'—for the seemingly fat-headed U.S. civilians. His fierce conviction is far removed from the gentle atmosphere of Regional A.I.D. Headquarters in Da Nang. But the A.I.D. people, too, have their point. Pacification cannot depend on the efforts of people like Colonel Corson, for such people are rare. There must be an established bureaucracy for agricultural credits and aid, for public health work, refugee organization and education. Like all bureaucracies it will be open to error and graft but this kind of work is best left to civilian experts.

The differences between the military and the civilians are more matters of personal pride than of principle. There is no real argument about 'how to win the hearts and minds of the people'. In both groups you find people who favour more and less reliance on Vietnamese; more and less private enterprise; more and less free handouts. The Marine Colonel Corson differs from U.S.A.I.D. in Da Nang almost exclusively in his attitude to the land question. He believes that the rents and tax on rice are so bad that the peasants must find other kinds of work. The U.S.A.I.D. men play down the problem of rent and tax and try to concentrate on improving the rice yield. The regional U.S.A.I.D. chief, Marcus J. Gordon, told me that credit was more of a problem than land reform. His assistant William Johnson, who runs the agricultural section, agreed that land reform was a problem but added: 'Hell, even in your country, if you own five-hundred acres of land you're not going to be too pleased if somebody wants to chop it up. It's not fair to moralize when it's their [the landlords'] pocket-book that's being hit. Maybe it isn't altogether a good thing to split up the land into small plots. Who are we to interfere in a free government? The Vietcong have given the peasants imposing-looking deeds to their land. We know that these documents don't mean anything but there are people who say we should carry out the V.C. policy of giving land to the peasants. But can we adopt the enemy's programme?' A good question.

*   *   *

From Da Nang I flew north to Hué which is always described in the news-agency stories as Vietnam's 'ancient and imperial capital', because the emperors lived here before the French conquest in the early nineteenth century. The River of Perfumes cuts Hué in two parts and of course its name is a subject of fun to the foreigners who have visited the place. The Americans, just like the French before them, say that the perfume is really of human dung swept down from the primitive drains of the city. In fact the river does have a pleasant smell. There is no industry in Hué to pollute the waters. The human dung, if it reaches the stream, is swept away by the current. If you lean over the bridge, you get a pleasant musty smell of mud and lotos and water weed.

Hué is a university city, like other university cities it has a rowing set—but here the rowers are girls who are not very proficient with either the long oars or the sliding seats. As a result they often send the boats spinning round in circles, but this very helplessness makes them attractive. They slip off the seats; their long hair falls about their knees; the splash of their ill-managed oars dampens their white *ao dais*. When things go badly wrong and the skiffs are in danger of sinking, the girls abandon ship and slide, with tresses hanging behind them, into the River of Perfumes, where they strike out in the breast-stroke—the loveliest method of swimming for women.

Standing on the bridge one day, I watched two herdsmen taking a dozen water buffaloes across the river. The men wore solar topees but their bodies were almost invisible in the dark water. The buffaloes swam with only their muzzles above the water. The journey took nearly half an hour because the front buffalo persisted in heading downstream while the beast at the rear, with a small calf paddling at its flank, was just as keen to go upstream. The herdsmen clutched at the animals' necks and horns; they screamed abuse from under their solar topees. But all the noise and splashing did not disturb the fishermen who slept in their sampans round about.

In the hot summer months the people of Hué sometimes spend the night in a sampan in order to get the benefit of the river breeze. These

Hué sampans, just like the Venetian gondolas which they resemble, have a romantic and even erotic reputation. Young girls and restless wives will do things in a sampan, so it is said, that they would not so much as contemplate on dry land. As a consequence Hué has a naughty reputation throughout the rest of Vietnam. Scandalous stories from Hué are popular with the newspapers in Saigon. In August last year, for example, the English-language *Saigon Daily News* began a story from Hué: 'A southern country boy whose local girl fiancée talked him into spending a pre-betrothal night aboard a sampan on this romantic city's lovely River of Perfumes barely escaped from his breeches, according to reliable sources here.' The young man, an army sergeant, had met the 'Hué lass' in Saigon. She told him that before getting married it would be necessary for both of them to go to Hué and receive her parents' permission. She persuaded him to go north, bringing his money and valuables with him. Since it was late when they arrived, they spent the night on one of the sampans that serve as floating hotels. Here, in the words of the *Saigon Daily News*, 'the soldier had such an exhaustingly good time with his girl friend that he fell into a deep slumber' or, as the *Vietnam Guardian* described the event, 'that night for the first time she did not refuse anything to him who immediately fell sound asleep after proving his virility repeatedly.' He woke to find the girl, seventy thousand piastres and his jewellery had all vanished and he was last seen, according to the *News* report, 'boarding an airport bus downtown, tears streaming from his eyes and regaling all within ear range of his one-night 70,000-piastre marriage'. The story, which may well be true, expresses the prejudice of the southerners against the people of Hué.

Southerners sometimes refer to Hué as the City of the Dead. The emperors who ruled there were oppressive towards their subjects and Hué, like all cities that now are not so powerful as they once were, appears rather melancholy to outsiders. The inhabitants are credited with peculiar and not very attractive characteristics. It is said that they make a display of poverty even when they are rich. It is said that they are proud and snobbish. The Diem family came from Hué, which is yet another grievance against the city. The Americans are unpopular here because they supported the Ky government against the militant Buddhists early in 1966. The burned-out wreck of the American Library is a testament to this hatred. I felt conscious of this hostility when I walked through the streets of Hué and when I tried to strike up acquaintanceships. It was no good explaining that I was English. The Vietnamese are very quick to distinguish between different types of foreigners—they would normally see from my clothes, haircut and manner that I was not American—but the people of Hué appear to dislike the English with special feeling because of what they regard as unfair references to the city on B.B.C. overseas broadcasts.

Hué is indeed a beautiful city, but only for one hour a day—at sunrise and sunset, when the soft light brings out the colour in river and trees and stone. When the sun is up, all colour is drained from the landscape. The river gives off a harsh chromium glare; the trees look dusty, and the stone has a flat pallid texture. The view over the river is oppressive except for the flag of South Vietnam—in orange and yellow stripes like a marzipan cake—that flutters over the citadel. The usual raucous loud-speaker plays 'Cheek to Cheek'; the usual barbed wire is draped along the riverside; and the usual children run up behind the foreigner to shout abuse and punch him in the small of the back.

I had brought with me a tourist brochure for Hué which caused considerable merriment to the locals. 'Look at that hotel they advertise here,' said one with derision. 'Go to the Tourist Office and ask for a room there. They have built the hotel but never opened it. They haven't even installed electricity yet. And look at all those ruins they advertise. Minh Mang's tomb? Impossible! It's controlled by the Vietcong. Gia Long's tomb? Impossible. It's also controlled by the Vietcong. The Khai Dinh tomb? That's possible. But who wants to go and see it? It was built in the nineteen-twenties.' I met an American who worked as a photographer for one of the glossy magazines and had been sent to prepare a feature on Hué as part of some series on great historic cities. He too had found difficulty in getting shots of the ancient monuments. However, the friendly army enabled him to take pictures of Gia Long's tomb by first mounting a one-hundred-and-fifty-man assault on the whole area. When the journalist had completed his work, the troops retired to Hué; and the Vietcong presumably took charge once more of the hero's mortal remains.

The pleasant hotel in Hué has a sign in the lobby:

Important Advice. For keeping the orders and the security. Please passengers don't lead the cyclomen enter in the Hotel-room with you. The Managing.

Since 'the Managing' was in Saigon throughout my stay in Hué, and the only remaining member of the staff did not speak a foreign language, I never found out the meaning of the sign. Why on earth *should* a guest bring a cyclo-man into his room? However, since the ground floor of the hotel served as a brothel and since most of the girls and clients arrived for their trysts by cyclo, it may be that cyclo-men sometimes intruded into the hotel rooms to continue their bargaining. The upstairs rooms were quiet, cool and inviolate.

Hotel guests take their meals at the Hué Club—formerly *Cercle Sportif*—over the road. Although *Le Monde* and *France Soir* are still available in the library, this club has lost most of its old French glory. There is thick dust on the piano. The ceiling fans are still. The food has degenerated to horrible fish soup, bits of tinned pork, and omelettes washed down with American bottled sauces. The bar smells of old unwashed dishes and pots and pans. The club servants doze in the arm-chairs or eat snacks or join in the ceaseless games of billiards and snooker. The swimming pool is only half full and its rich, green water looks better suited to lotos-growing than swimming. At least half the two hundred members, so I was told, no longer pay their monthly sub-scriptions. This is not because they are short of money but rather because of Hué's traditional stinginess. The rich here, so this com-plainant said, have always worn simple black calico clothes like peasants in order to trick the tax collector. 'They like to come to the club to play tennis,' he went on; 'that's considered very chic and bourgeois. But they don't want to help keep up the court.'

This torpor was very agreeable after the frenzy of Saigon. It was pleasant to sit in the Hué Club drinking bottles of Tiger beer and watching the lizards on the walls. One evening, a pair of them started to copulate, upside down, on the ceiling. The male, in the heat of his ecstasy, lost his grip on the female and fell twenty feet to the ground. He got up, shook himself, uttered a rather groggy cry of *tac-tac*, then started to climb back up the wall to resume the fun. But what with the shock of his fall, or (like the soldier in the sampan) the effects of 'such an exhaustingly good time with his girl friend', he kept losing his grip and dropping down to the floor. By the time he at last reached the ceiling, the female had grown bored and disappeared.

One morning I felt sufficiently energetic to visit some friends of a friend on the other side of the river. I spoke to a Frenchman in the Hué

Club and asked how I should give the address to the cyclo-man. 'Just ask for Clemenceau Bridge,' he said. 'Officially now they've changed the name to Nguyen Hoang Bridge but everybody still calls it Clemenceau.' I walked out into the road where the heat made me feel limp and dizzy. I hailed a cyclo-man and told him to go to the Clemenceau Bridge and then turn right. He smiled and apologized but he had never heard of the Pont Clemenceau. I demonstrated by sign language where I wanted to go, which he readily understood, and then I took my place in the cyclo. The seat was covered by a piece of sacking that said: 'Yellow Corn Meal. Enriched. Degermed. Donated by the People of the United States of America. Not to be sold or exchanged.' I sat on it with pleasure.

I went to several meals with a family of Vietnamese who were under the care of a formidable mother. But I shall call her Mrs Hué rather than Madame Hué because she was delicate and sensitive and in no way like Madame Nhu. Her house, though, was built in the typically Vietnamese style. One entered it through the back of a shop and came immediately into a fine room with Chinese screens and the black-varnished low table which serves the Vietnamese as a bed of honour. The meals were of excellent quality and the conversation quiet and restrained. It is bad form in Vietnam to talk loudly or to display any grossness of thought or imagination. Whispered platitudes and compliments are the approved form. All Mrs Hue's sons, daughters and cousins resembled her in their gentle, intelligent beauty. They were also rather reserved when the conversation came round to politics because, so I gathered, two or three of the family were in prison or exile for having taken part in anti-government riots. Even the motherly Mrs Hué was bitter about the political situation. 'I try to learn English,' she said in French, 'but I just don't like the Americans. I saw a film the other day which showed some dead American soldiers who had been killed fighting here in Vietnam. I felt touched—but all the same I don't like them.'

A son of about eighteen and his school-friend offered to take us on a tour of the old city of Hué which stretches for about a mile square on the north side of the city. They provided us with bicycles which were many sizes too small for Europeans, and hard to steer in the hurly-burly of Vietnamese traffic. We quickly reached the Imperial City, which now serves as a park and pleasure-ground for the people of Hué.

The oldest of the palaces and the monuments date to the beginning of the nineteenth century and the reign of the great emperor Gia Long who reunited all Vietnam under his rule. The architecture is dignified rather than thrilling. The buildings are low, stocky and finished in dark wood. They have overhanging wooden roofs and thick wooden pillars in front. There are batteries of old cannons, many painted wooden lions and several lakes clogged with lotos flowers. The imperial lawns are now rather bald and mangy; the unspeakable barbed wire has been left around in the gardens. But the general impression is peaceful. The students of Hué University like the Imperial City. You see them poring over their textbooks beside the pools and on the parapets by the Ngo Mon gate. A spooning couple, both in uniform, peeped at us shyly from under the shade of a carved dragon. The students have left their graffiti upon the outer walls of the citadel. There are algebraic signs, a few political slogans and fleeting, allusive fragments of French: '*Liberté. Qu'est-ce que c'est?*' and the even more poignant '*Amour?*'. These fragments seem typical of the shy and melancholy students we met. Many have been arrested for demonstrating against the government. Most of them will have to join the army at twenty-three and stand a good chance of getting killed in the war.

They are troubled young people who take their rest by Tinh Tam, the Lake of Serenity of Heart.

* * *

The South Korean Tiger Division controls a large area of the hinterland behind Qui Nhon on the east coast. I was curious to see how the Vietnamese population regarded their fellow Asians and in what ways the Korean presence was different from the American and I therefore went to stay at the Tiger H.Q. about ten miles inland from the city of Qui Nhon. 'Our camp used to be V.C. territory,' one of the R.O.K. (Republic of Korea) officers told me. 'Then we came and they all escaped or were killed.' The provinces to the north and south are almost entirely controlled by the Vietcong but the Tigers' T.A.O.R. (Tactical Area of Responsibility) is 'reconsolidated'. The Koreans say that the local population controlled by the Vietcong has fallen from 97,000 to 4,000 and that the American Air Force has sprayed poison on thousands of acres of woodland and crops which might provide shelter or food to the enemy. The blackened hill-sides and patches of valley present an unpleasant contrast to the green, rolling countryside—like patches of leprosy on a human body. As a result of the military clearing operation performed in 1965, it is now possible to move about the territory in a Jeep. The remaining Vietcong seldom appear by day and seldom lay mines in the road. There are many Korean patrols and sentries who give one a brisk salute and a cry of 'Urrh!' which, so I was told, is the Korean word for tiger.

The R.O.K. troops wear kepi helmets which are the cause of some nasty comparisons with the Foreign Legion. An Englishman likened the role of the R.O.K. in South Vietnam to the role of the Gurkhas in Malaysia. But the R.O.K. are more popular than were the Gurkhas who came here in 1945 and appalled the Vietnamese by their savage conduct. One of the first things one notices in the Koreans is their cheerfulness. It has been observed that Koreans divide into two psychological types: those who always smile and those who always scowl. The Koreans I met here were mostly smilers. They had a relaxed expression such as one does not often find in the Vietnamese or American soldiers. They are also stupendously fit. Their broad shoulders and short, bandy legs make them look squat but in fact they are much taller as well as stockier than the Vietnamese. It would no more be possible to mistake a Vietnamese for a Korean than to mistake either for an American. The R.O.K. troops have borrowed the American device of a name-badge worn on the chest; but since most Koreans seem to be called Kim, the badges were not of much help.

The Tiger Division's camp is clean, neat and well disciplined, offering good food spiced with some hot Korean sauce. After work the officers play tennis while private soldiers fetch the balls and shout the score: 'Love-u fifteen, Love-u thirty'. In the evening I drank Pepsi-Cola in the Sergeants' Mess and listened to Christmas carols on the loudspeaker. One evening some of the N.C.O.s invited me to the outdoor film show. The film was called *Combat* and it described the attack by an American platoon on a German artillery battery in France during the Second World War. Since the film was in English, without Korean subtitles, the audience understood very little beyond the scenes of skirmishing and artillery fire. But they watched with great patience as the captured American sergeant tried to win over his German captor ('I played oboe in the Berlin State Orchestra') and they stirred with interest in the final reel as the sergeant, accompanied by the oboist, overcame the Nazi officers and destroyed the German positions. Next morning the Tigers showed me their 'booty room' of captured Vietcong weapons and supplies. There were Russian and American rifles, home-made booby traps, portraits of Ho Chi Minh, tubes of toothpaste, and plastic solar topees. There is one rare find which the Koreans consider very funny—a manual of baby care for the use of Vietcong mothers. The drawings are primitive so that the baby appears much too fat, as in renaissance paintings.

On the second day I was invited to the Tiger Division briefing room where a colonel rattled off his progress report of martial and civil victories. A private soldier stood to attention beside him throughout the half-hour recital in order to turn over the charts, maps and 'visual aids'. The colonel described some of the military measures taken against the Vietcong and explained some of the Vietcong tactics they had to face, including 'the employment of graveyards as cover to snipe from in spite of the local population's complaint of annoyance because of the insult to ancestor worship'. Some of the Vietcong had hidden in holes in the ground with entrances only thirty centimetres wide 'which makes it difficult even for the average R.O.K. soldier to get inside'.

Last but not least, or rather 'rast but not reast', the colonel explained the 'civic and psy-op work'. With a truly American zest for statistics and progress charts, he recounted the Tiger achievements: 8,652 donations of rice; 66,728 patients treated; 145,382 gifts such as calendars to promote an understanding of Korean culture; Tiger Division band concerts; 'sister village' schemes and 'Elders Respect Parties'. He was very disturbed by the story that had appeared a few weeks before in *Time Magazine* saying that R.O.K. troops had flayed a Vietcong prisoner in revenge for atrocities to a Korean. 'There is no truth whatsoever in these stories that we have taken people's skin off,' he assured me. He said that villagers in the north of the Tiger area had begged to be occupied by the Koreans rather than by ARVIN. Civilians in Qui Nhon had paraded with banners asking the R.O.K. to stay until the end of pacification. Or so he said. I could not find a Vietnamese who had witnessed this parade. Another information officer said that the good deeds of the R.O.K. had even made themselves felt on the enemy. 'The Vietcong propaganda says that the Tiger Division is on the side of the Vietcong and not of the Republic of Vietnam. It says that the U.S.

cannot win because the V.C. are too strong; that the Korean soldiers came to Vietnam to liberate them from the Americans.' I asked him why he thought the Vietcong should use such an improbable line of propaganda. He replied: 'Because the Korean soldiers are doing very kindly things to the Vietnamese. We have never shown any cruel deed to them. This is the V.C. way of explaining the kindness of the Korean soldiers.'

During the next few days, I had a chance to inspect some of the R.O.K. 'psy-op'. First I was taken to Cu Mong pass on the southern boundary of the Korean T.A.O.R. The Tigers hold the pass itself and the hills rising above it. The valley, which slopes down through hilly scrub to paddy fields and a long plain used to be Vietcong territory and Korean patrols would not attempt to cross it. With field-glasses you could see the Vietcong blockposts along the winding road that leads down from the pass. The Americans had bombed these block-posts and other targets south of Cu Mong but the Korean ground forces had not tried to invade. A few months later, the Americans and Koreans fought their way into the valley, but this whole region is still sharply contested.

The Cu Mong pass is the traditional market-place for trade between Qui Nhon and the valley beyond. The Koreans have allowed these markets to start again even though it means trading with the enemy. 'This market between free-world Vietnam and V.C. Vietnam would not be permitted by South Vietnam troops,' said a R.O.K. officer. 'It is illegal, but we believe that not all the people in Communist held territory are Communists.' Their motives are not simply humanitarian. They hope to gain intelligence and even defectors at the market place. Above all they want to perform their 'psy-op'.

The markets are held each morning. Women from Qui Nhon arrive by Lambretta mini-bus to sell rice, salt, joss sticks, baby food, paper and cheap factory-made goods. Women from Vietcong territory come on foot up the road to sell coconut oil, pineapples, fish and crabs. The trade goes on against a background of psy-op. The Koreans hand out propaganda leaflets, deliver propaganda addresses over the loud-speaker and chat to individual visitors from the Communist zone. They give a present of rice to each woman, and a Tiger medical team gives medicine and advice to anybody who needs it. The orderlies smear salve on the barbed-wire wounds of a woman, dole out a pill to an old man with a pain in his back, and utter a sympathetic cluck to a woman with raging toothache. There is no dentist. The officer in command at the market that day said: 'We tell the troops that they must be very kindly towards the Vietnamese.' He himself gave a very kindly look at a girl in a mollusc hat. The Koreans are endlessly fascinated by these hats. They examine with interest how the women pour rice in and out of the hats, which act as a unit of measurement. They guffawed with joy when a pretty girl filled her hat under a tap and then drank from the brim.

The Koreans are equally proud of their 'psy-op' at Hou Thanh, in the north of the T.A.O.R., where Korean artillerymen have helped the Vietnamese to build a dam that will water otherwise unproductive land during the dry season. The Koreans supplied the engineering knowledge and most of the cement. Moreover Korean troops worked next to the villagers in the physical job of excavation. I saw them standing up to the waist in water, with an intense sun beating down on their steel helmets. It struck me as typical of Korean fortitude that they should wear heavy helmets when straw hats would have been more comfortable and more effective.

The officers at the dam spoke with strong American accents and even their attitudes were American. The colonel was mightily pleased at how he had got the work going in spite of opposition from desk wallahs in Qui Nhon and A.I.D. Headquarters. 'The noise of these pile-drivers,' he said with great satisfaction, 'was heard as far as Saigon.' He was also pleased with his own naughtiness at having 'scrounged' the metal needed for the dam. I asked if the villagers were working as volunteers. The colonel said that the dam was in their own interest. 'They have two leaders in the village whom they follow blindly. One is an old man and spiritual teacher. The other is young and full of inspiration. They follow these men, and although they could get more money elsewhere they are content with the five kilos of rice a day that we give them.' The colonel believed that the Vietnamese way of thinking was similar to the Korean, which was why he had organized Elders Respect Parties to win the confidence of the old people—the people who really mattered. He was very pleased with the good effect that the dam had made on the happiness of the village. 'When we first came here the people never smiled. They were quite expressionless. Now they come up and greet us and talk to us.' He regarded the

Vietnamese with patronizing benevolence. 'Our soldiers who come from the country were amazed at seeing land which could produce three or four rice crops a year. Ours only produces one. But we think some of their methods of agriculture are rather primitive. And we think the Vietnamese do not work very hard.' It is the universal cry of the northerner; a Prussian would say the same thing in southern Italy.

Another artillery unit had built some pig pens for its 'sister village', Nam Tang, and I went to see the official opening ceremony. 'Each village near a Korean unit must have a sister relationship,' one of the officers explained, 'so that if any villagers get any information about the V.C., they bring this information immediately to their sister unit.' The top Tiger officers and a U.S.A.I.D. man were given garlands to wear and Seven-Up to sip. The A.I.D. man inspected the pig pens and said: 'This is a very important step you have taken. This is a very important progress.' The Tiger band, in gleaming steel helmets, played a medley of Vietnamese and Korean tunes; a storeman handed out bags of rice stamped with a tiger's head and presented bright blue uniforms to the local police force. Some sad-looking village girls did a folk-dance, followed by three young men in shabby uniforms who acted the legendary battle between the Dragon and the Fairy. The Koreans and Americans were looking pleased as punch and had themselves photographed with the folk-dancers. The American was particularly satisfied with the newly purchased pigs—'Notice how well they stand. Not like those Vietnamese pigs whose bellies trail on the ground.' It is nobler to give than to receive—and also much more fun. The beaming good humour and confidence that one saw in the faces of the Koreans and the Americans was not matched on the faces of the villagers, who looked bored and unhappy. Many were refugees from battle areas who had been settled there rather against their will. The Koreans, just like the Americans, say that South Vietnam would soon be victorious if only the Vietnamese were 'more highly motivated'. They want to infuse motivation like petrol into a tank. Perhaps the South Koreans too lacked 'motivation' after their war. Perhaps if South Vietnam conquers its Communists and enters the American camp, it too will one day send a free-world force to motivate the South Burmese or the South Malaysians. The Tiger Division's Methodist chaplain, Kim, said of the Vietnamese: 'They are very naive so that sometimes I feel ashamed. They are very kind, but they do not say what they believe even when they have convictions. They remain expressionless.' The South Koreans find the South Vietnamese inscrutable.

Anyone who visits the Tiger Division will be obliged to witness some demonstrations of Tae Kwon Do, which is a kind of karate performed as a group exercise. All the R.O.K. troops practise for half an hour a day and many take a month's full-time course to become experts. There were at this time 278 'black belts' and more than 10,000 brown and green belts serving in South Vietnam. The troops train barefooted in calf-length white pyjamas or rolled-up fatigue trousers. The instructor roars the commands and the whole platoon punches and turns and kicks as one man. One action looks as though a cricket fielder had picked up a ball on the boundary, leaned back to throw, then suddenly swivelled to kick a spectator's teeth in. With each forward thrust the squad lets out a blood-curdling roar. When the mass drill is over, the squad divides into pairs that practise the various throws and falls. And after the drill is over, they are very eager to show any visitors their more sensational party tricks. A sergeant, looking like Ian Fleming's Oddjob, broke through five thick tiles with a thrust of his outstretched fingers. Another chopped four heaped bricks with the side of his hand, and a third broke five bricks with a butt of the forehead. Afterwards, to the great glee of the troop, the officer compared the sergeant's hand with mine. The sergeant's looked like the hoof of a rhinoceros; mine like a lazy civilian's hand. I grinned to show that I understood how comic this difference was.

The Koreans, as part of their psy-op, give courses of Tae Kwon Do to the Vietnamese in Qui Nhon. Squads of ARVIN, policemen and students practise every night in the stadium under the guidance of Korean instructors. Although Tae Kwon Do is in theory adapted to every physique, the Vietnamese look very frail for this bone-crushing business, and their witty view of life prevents them from taking it quite so seriously as the Koreans do. The violent, crude gestures do not suit these graceful, delicate people. One notices this particularly in the squad of Qui Nhon High School girls who practise the art in a court-yard by the sea. They obviously lacked the savage spirit of Tae Kwon Do, for they giggled and chattered throughout the lesson. The savage Korean battle-grunt was transformed in their pretty mouths to a soft cry of 'yes'. Their boy-friends stood at the side to crack jokes and try to make the girls blush. This behaviour angered the black-belt R.O.K.

officer who stood at my side. After glaring at the girls he turned to me with a growling comment: 'They do it like a dance!' So might a Rugby international feel if he saw women playing at Twickenham.

I doubt whether Tae Kwon Do will help the Free World Forces to win in South Vietnam, although it may be useful at close range. One sergeant instructor, who screwed up his eyes in a sinister way and spoke in a hoarse whisper, explained to me: 'Maybe I wants to kick the heart. I kick the heart. Maybe I wants to kick the stomach. I kick the stomach. Maybe I wants to hurt a man. I hurt him. Maybe I wants to make him fall down. I make him fall down. Maybe I wants to kill him. I kill him.' A major told me that he had never actually used Tae Kwon Do in combat but it was useful 'if someone attacked you in a dark street.' Such an attack is more likely in peaceful America than in South Vietnam.

One afternoon I was watching a group of artillerymen as they practised their Tae Kwon Do when a special order was given and they all rushed—still wearing pyjamas—to load their guns. I imagined that this was a standard drill to keep them alert and ready for action at any time of day. To my surprise and with great pain to my nervous system, they fired off a rapid volley of 105 howitzer shells. I asked, rather astonished, if this was a part of the training, for the shells had fallen a couple of miles away in the very direction from which I had just come. The officer, a smiling Kim, explained that they were firing at the Viet-cong, who, I should imagine, have much more respect for howitzer shells than karate chops.

The heartiness of the Tiger Division contrasts with the misery of the Vietnamese in their area. The provinces round about have been a centre of heavy fighting ever since the start of the Vietminh struggle in 1946. Hundreds of thousands of refugees have come into Qui Nhon to escape the fighting, the bombing and the political feuds. At the same time Qui Nhon itself is a major port and operational base for the R.O.K. and the U.S. Armies, so that the old social structure has still further suffered from the inflation and uproar of a war economy. The city is uglier and even more maimed in spirit than Da Nang to the north. Bulldozers chew up the ground; scoops dredge up the sea bed; dynamite erodes the hills around. The whole area has been swallowed up and masticated in an immense industrial maw and will shortly be spat out again on the sea shore. The great American trucks belch their black vapour into the humid, hot air where it liquefies in a film of sooty phlegm. The shacks look more decrepit, the bars smell stronger of sweat and carbolic than anywhere else in Vietnam. Here I saw the barbed wire horror brought to its final lunacy. There were strands of it wrapped round a young tree, like streamers round a maypole. The wire could serve no possible purpose. There were no bullocks to lean against the tree. Anybody who wanted to chop it down could simply remove the wire.

In order to see some of the refugee camps I called at the Province Headquarters and spoke to Mr Nguyen Dien, who is responsible for their welfare. He had been trained in one of the anti-Communist cadre schools and he was full of 'motivation'. The refugees problem, he thought, was caused by the fact that peasants were 'ignorant, unsophisticated people—not like us—and very easily used (roulé) by the Communists.' He meant, I think, that many refugees were fleeing not from Communism but from the war and did not want to take part in 'new village' schemes. Many refugees are very reluctant to join the 'new villages'. The overwhelming majority, so I was told by neutral social workers, are refugees from American bombing rather than from the Vietcong.

Most of the refugees now live in two camps run by the Roman Catholics. The largest of these, known as the 'old camp', is one of the most disgusting spectacles I have ever seen. The squat shacks are pressed tight together. The alleys between are covered in dirt and excrement, and guarded by snarling, wounded mongrels who bare their teeth at the intruder in yellow, ulcerous snarls. Filthy, pot-bellied and naked children approach you with one hand clutched over the groin and the other held out in greeting or supplication. There may be misery as bad as this in Calcutta or Hong Kong but it comes as a shock in such a rich country as Vietnam. The Americans, with staggering bad taste, have taken a residential site next to the 'old camp' and set up huge metal caravans, each equipped with air-conditioning, cooking, bathing and toilet appliances. These gleaming, splendid homes are distributed over the site with decent space between each so that the population density must be about one hundredth that of the 'old camp'.

After seeing the two Roman Catholic camps I went to the Buddhist camp by the sea outside the city. Perhaps because of some European prejudice, I had expected this to be the worst of the three. On the contrary, it was the smartest refugee camp I have ever seen. The huts were made of corrugated aluminium and floored with smooth cement. Each was clean and sweet-smelling. Each had its hammock and wooden beds, its carved shrine, joss sticks and offertory fruit. (Bananas are favourite because, so the Vietnamese believe, the Buddha was fond of bananas during his time on earth.) The children were clean, well dressed and did not beg—although when they prodded my ample stomach and jeered 'chop-chop' I thought harsh things about the Buddhist sense of humour. Whenever we stopped at a hut the house-holder would put on a clean shirt before greeting us. These Buddhist refugees work as fishermen, even although many come from inland villages. Many foreigners, and I was guilty of this, are inclined to underrate the Buddhists because of their querulous politics and their odd, giggling manner. This camp was a testament to the strength of the Buddhist culture and the leadership of the bonzes.

I chanced to be at the Catholic 'old camp' when they were moving two lorry-loads of the refugees into one of the 'new villages' of the interior. Furniture, clothes, shrines, food and people were heaped on to the lorry in a gigantic kedgeree. One could see in the eyes of the refugees a terrible sense of fatigue at having to make yet another journey, to set up another home, to take another risk on the political future. I have never seen people so depressed, so totally lacking in 'motivation'. The refugees to whom I talked had only one real wish— to return home, meaning their own home on the patch of land from which they came. Ignorant, unsophisticated people the director of refugees had called them. The Koreans and the Americans also find the refugees irritating. They cannot understand their apathy and weariness, their inability to make the best of the situation. When I was in the Ghenh Rang camp, the newer and better of those run by the Catholics, a lorry drew up outside and a tall American lieutenant entered. He had brought a pile of wood that he wanted to offer to the refugees. The wood was free, he explained, he knew it would come in useful, so would they simply let him know where they wanted it dumped? The director of the camp and his deputy, as well as two men from the Province H.Q., were all in the offices at the time but none of them wanted to take the wood. They did not have the people to unload the wood. They did not know where to unload it. They did not know whether the wood was necessary. And so the excuses tumbled out. Yet it was quite clear that the wood was necessary. The children in the

E

camp had to sit on the floor of the schoolrooms because there was no furniture. Any wood was invaluable as supports for the shacks in rough weather. Moreover the lieutenant had a tip truck and therefore it would not be necessary to get people to do the unloading. The lieutenant asked me to translate his offer into French, although I felt sure that the officials had well understood his English. Their problems, I imagine, were psychological. For one thing, they had all no doubt discerned some astrological reasons for not taking the wood. 'The lorry is pointing south. Doesn't he know that's unlucky?' 'He's a Negro and my horoscope said to avoid the colour black?' 'It's bad to accept gifts under the sign of the fish.' These astrological obstacles can be used by the Vietnamese to impede any kind of action, though normally, if they are feeling happy and confident, they do not worry about the stars. But refugees, whether Vietnamese or Europeans, are predisposed, by the nature of their condition, to resist help, suspect generosity and avoid action.

I made friends with a shopkeeper who spoke good French and kept insisting I drank some rot-gut brew he had bought as White Horse whisky. Although his business was doing well and he had little to fear from the war or politics, he was the glummest man I met in Qui Nhon. 'What this country needs,' he would say, 'is a *maître*. We have *chefs* and *patrons* but we need a *maître*.' He disliked all sides in the Vietnam war. 'The Americans profit from it, both the Republicans and the Democrats. And the Russians, and the Chinese. If there was ever peace here in Vietnam, the two sides, the capitalists and the Communists, would find somewhere else to fight their war, maybe in Thailand or Indonesia. All right! But why can't they leave *us* in peace at last?'

When you listen to the psy-op briefings given by the Americans or the Koreans or the Australians, and then listen to the Vietnamese, you are struck by one supreme difference. The outsiders are eager and energetic. The Vietnamese do not care very much any more. The French, Japanese, Chinese, British, Americans, Australians and now Koreans have all lorded it here during the last twenty years. Perhaps the Japanese were the most liked. The Koreans, now, are not unpopular. But the Vietnamese are tired of them all.

Chapter Three SAIGON

FROM TIME TO TIME, IN SAIGON, I WOULD GO FOR AN EVENING of smoking opium. The den I patronized was the upstairs room of a tradesman living in Cholon, the Chinese quarter. On the first occasion we arrived at about nine and were welcomed into a typical bourgeois Buddhist family's front hall with a garish portrait of the God on the right-hand wall. The host's wife and children were sleeping in their pyjamas on the big bed by the foot of the stairs. The upstairs room, where the smokers gathered, was cut in two by a screen of dirty blankets and most of the floor space was occupied by one of the low, wide tables that serve the Vietnamese as beds. Some of the smokers lay on the bed but late-comers settled down on the clean linoleum floor. The room was decorated with a small Buddhist shrine and a photographic calendar from a company that makes excavating machinery. Most smokers rest their head on a Vietnamese pillow, which is a wooden box with a sloping side. Whenever I tried to use one I got a crick in the neck, but the linoleum felt cool and the atmosphere was relaxing. One of the old-time smokers apologized for the den. In the days before opium was forbidden there were most luxurious establishments where you lay on cushioned sofas and feasted your eyes on beautiful paintings. After the ban it had been difficult to re-establish contact with the *patrons*. One smoker told me: 'At first I did not know anywhere until the Brazilian Ambassador showed me. He knew of three places— imagine that! The Brazilian Ambassador! And I'm a Vietnamese!'

There were normally about eight to twelve smokers, all men. Several were officers in the army of South Vietnam but I did not realize this until afterwards as they followed the opium fashion of stripping down to their underwear. The smokers lay on their backs, with knees raised in the posture that gives the greatest sense of relaxation. Sometimes they lay with legs straddling each others' bodies or even with legs interlocked—like puppies in a basket. The Vietnamese appear to

enjoy physical contact with one another even when there is no sexual significance to the touch. One man, who perhaps took more pipes than was good for him, always lay flat on his back with his legs stiffly outstretched and his forearms propped in the air quite rigid from elbow to fingertips. He would lie like this for half an hour in a state of paralytic trance, until, all of a sudden, one of his toes would give a convulsive twitch. Most of the smokers have packets of cigarettes and transistor radio sets within easy reach on the floor beside them.

The *patron* liked to prepare the first pipe for his guests before handing the job to an underling. He was a middle-aged man with thick grey hair swept back from a high, intelligent forehead. He had an ascetic, puritan look which no doubt came from the opium addict's malnutrition. His arms were so thin that his gold watch-strap hung an inch loose from his wrist. He seemed to take a great joy in the actual job of rolling the opium pellet and pushing it into the small hole in the wooden bowl. He lay in the traditional posture with one foot resting on the calf of the other leg.

When the Diem regime outlawed the smoking of opium, the police seized and destroyed most of the fine wooden pipes in use at the dens. The modern smoker has to make do with a length of plastic tube attached to the primitive wooden bowl. Others have a plastic pipe about three feet long with a short tube fixed near one end. These instruments look like a narcotic oboe. The opium fans (or *amateurs* as they say in French) do not mind the ugly apparatus that has replaced the traditional pipes, but they do complain about the poor quality of the opium itself. Ah! they sighed, for the old days when the *fumeries* were legal. You got two pipes to the gramme in those days instead of four or five. It was so delicious that if one smoked a pipe here in the room they could sniff it out in the street. But this stuff you got nowadays was blended with all kinds of rubbish. To get the real thing you would have to visit India or Laos. All these smokers revere Laos, the legendary garden of opium where, so they believe, you can still visit a legal *fumerie*. As a matter of fact smoking is now illegal even in Laos but that country certainly grows the stuff and exports it. Smugglers from Laos drop bundles of opium from aeroplanes into the highlands of South Vietnam, where it is treated and blended and sold to the cities. However, the local officials and maybe the Vietcong have exacted a tax on this trade. The overheads are excessive and the risks too great. As a result, only poor stuff reaches the *fumeries* where it is sold at about two shillings a pipe. The habitual smoker will pay this price and still smoke ten pipes in an evening. Ten pipes, each smoked in one deep inhalation; the smoking itself takes only a minute in all.

You hear all sorts of clever epigrams about opium in Vietnam. They say, for example, that opium is the religion of the people or that opium is the opium of the people. Whatever the social effects of this drug, there is nothing depraved or even singular about the circumstances in which it is taken. The atmosphere of an opium den has its nearest English equivalent in the pub. There is the same initial small-talk and platitude; the same opportunity for self-expression, boasting and fantasy. The *patron* of this den was like a certain type of opinionated landlord. He had strong views about what he read in the evening newspapers. He was rather grumpy and very much a character. As he kneaded the opium on the side of the bowl he would grumble about the latest attacks on North Vietnam, the ignorance of MacNamara and the craziness of women. One evening he told the company that his wife had just done a bunk (*foutu le camp*) and this provoked a half-hour of cracker-barrel philosophy from the guests. One older man recalled the story about a sea captain's wife who had traced her husband to his rendezvous with an unknown mistress and how she had called in the chief of police to break down the door and confront the guilty pair— only to find her husband in bed with the wife of the chief of police. The same man was fond of stories of premonition. A brother and sister dreamed that someone was going to murder them and throw them under a bridge in Saigon. The police were called in just in time to stop a wicked relative from killing the children's aunt and putting her under a bridge. Everyone says that these stories of premonition are utterly Vietnamese in character; they sound like the ghost stories told after dinner in middle-class English homes.

A gloomy schoolteacher was one of the regulars at the den. He once announced himself as 'a troubador born after his time' and he had the morose frown and bright eyes of a real poet. Every day, so he told me, he contemplated suicide because of the torments he suffered due to his too-intense imagination. Why did the junior teachers at his school get paid less than him? Why were the people of South Vietnam so obsessed by the pursuit of dollars? 'We have fallen completely under the influence of capitalism,' he used to say, 'but we fear what would happen if the Vietcong were to take over. What would happen to my school? What would happen to your newspaper?' 'And what would happen to your opium?' I added.

Towards the end of the evening, conversation came back to the great days of opium before the war and to the great opium countries of Laos and India. 'When things get desperate I come here to get calm,' the sad schoolteacher said. The *amateurs* say that opium is the best antidote to the war. On my first evening in the den, very soon after coming to Vietnam, I was startled by a loud explosion outside. 'Thunder?' I asked, and one of the smokers said: 'No, mortars.' Later in the evening, when I had smoked several pipes, an even louder explosion shook the buildings. 'Mortars?' I asked with a casual drawl. 'No, thunder,' the answer came back, and really it did not matter any more.

But the enormous prevalence of opium-smoking in South Vietnam cannot really be blamed on the war. The Vietnamese smoked almost as much in the peace between the two world wars. The Chinese of peaceful Hong Kong are even more avid and desperate addicts. The Americans, who themselves are so prone to narcotics, have not taken to opium in South Vietnam. Those who told me that they had tried it did not enjoy it. The American *amateurs* prefer pot or L.S.D. from Hong Kong or Laos.

Vietnamese women sometimes tell you that men who smoke opium will produce crippled or handicapped babies. It is a euphemistic justification for women's more accurate fear that opium makes men impotent.

Some *amateurs* say that the real pleasure of opium starts several hours after you finish smoking. The smell and taste are mildly pleasant; they reminded me of a certain Indian restaurant near Leicester Square. The drug had no obviously evil effect except that it made me want to smoke cigarettes. However, the dreams that followed were really remarkable.

Coleridge wrote 'Kubla Khan' under the influence of opium. The poem I wrote was merely a simple parody of American military and governmental language. The first two lines had occurred to me when I visited Operation Hastings and saw the Marine 'K.I.A.' I wrote the remaining lines at night after an evening of opium. The glossary has been added since.

Americans in Bar, Saigon.
Gerald Scarfe – Vietnam.

The heavy contact now is o'er,
   The K.I.A. are laid to rest;
The sun now re-initiates
   De-escalation in the west.
Brave COMUS in his Saigon tent
   Prepares his daily B.D.A.;
While heli-lifted MEDIVAC
   Extracts the W.I.A.

The CHICOM fear our cushioned troops,
   The N.V.N. from ARVIN flee;
While VEENAF, twenty clicks away,
   Pre-strikes within the Dee Em Zee.
The Civic Action now begins
   As friends and former foe relate;
The psy-op cadres, hopefully,
   Will start to reconsolidate.

Their highly motivated PATS
   Rout out the infrastructural Reds.
The reconstructed peasants sleep
   Upon their A.I.D.-assisted beds.
Now shout hurrah for R & R!
   For 35 and 33!
Let Slope and My together cry:
   'Dash down yon cup of Saigon Tea!'

The following glossary should explain most of the terms used.

Heavy Contact: a big battle.
K.I.A.: Killed in Action.
COMUS: General Westmoreland, Commander U.S. Forces in South Vietnam. He should strictly be called COMUS MACVEE (Commander U.S. Military Assistance Command Vietnam). The word 'tent' is poetic licence. COMUS MACVEE works in a large, heavily guarded and air-conditioned building in Saigon.
B.D.A.: Bomb Damage Assessment. These reports are a matter of great concern and controversy.
heli-lifted: lifted by helicopter.

MEDIVAC: Medical evacuation.
W.I.A.: Wounded in Action.
CHICOM: Communist China.
cushioned: augmented or reinforced.
N.V.N.: North Vietnam (troops).
VEENAF: South Vietnamese Air Force. Formerly commanded by Marshal Ky, later Prime Minister of South Vietnam.
clicks: kilometres.
pre-strikes: attacks by air preliminary to a ground attack.
Dee Em Zee: the de-militarized zone between North and South Vietnam. The Z is of course pronounced 'zee' in the American fashion. The zone is now militarized by both sides in the war.
Civic Action: social work designed to win over peasants to the government.
relate: to make friends with.
hopefully: meaning 'we hope', not, as in England, 'full of hope'.
reconsolidate: to win over from Communism.
highly motivated: an American sociological term meaning confident, brave or inspired. The Americans concede with regret that the Vietcong tend to be more highly motivated than the government supporters.
PATS: People's Action Teams of political police.
infrastructural: The Americans say that certain villages have a V.C. infrastructure. This can mean that one or two Vietcong live as agents in the village, or that the whole village is favourable to the Vietcong.
R & R; Rest and Recreation—local leave for American troops in cities like Hong Kong, Bangkok and Singapore. It is frequently called I & I, for intercourse and intoxication.
35: the Vietnamese astrological sign of the goat. It represents sexual virility. Bar girls flatter clients by telling them they are 35.
33: the name of the locally brewed beer.
Slope: a Vietnamese in American slang (from 'slopehead').
My: American (in Vietnamese). Compare Anh (Englishman), Phap (Frenchman).
Saigon Tea: Cold tea served at six shillings a glass to bar girls.

* * *

Many tailors and tourists shops in Tu Do, the main street of Saigon, offer displays of 'Stateside ribbons'. These are crudely designed and coloured badges, commemorating a stay in Vietnam, which the veteran can sew on to his coat when he goes back to America—or 'Stateside'. A civilian is puzzled by some of the legends referring to units or regiments. The Marine and Special Forces and First Division ribbons are easy to recognize, but what about 'Ruff n' Tuff', 'Ladrow's Loafers', or 'Suck out Lifer'? Some are ironic, like 'Sorry about that, Vietnam', or abrupt, like 'Go to Hell'. Many shops sell black leather jackets with maps of Indo-China superimposed on the back and the slogan: 'Every day I live with death. When I die the angels will take me to heaven'; or 'When I die I'll go to heaven because I've spent my time in hell. 65–66 Vietnam.' There is even a version for Puerto Rican and Mexican troops: 'Cuando yo muere sé que voy al ceilo. Porque ettuvo ya en al infierno.' Similar badges, I gather, were sold to American troops during the war in Korea. The favourite badge in Saigon and the most specifically Vietnamese is round, yellow, and four inches across. Three symbols appear in the centre: a label of 33 *Bière Export*, a rifle and a naked girl with open legs. The lettering round the sides reads: FIGHTERS BY TRADE. DRUNKARDS BY CHOICE. LOVERS BY NIGHT. SORRY BOUT THAT.' It is the simple fantasy of the eternal soldier. Unhappily for the Americans, those who do most of the fighting do not get much chance to drink beer or make love. Even those who spend their time in Saigon and the other cities seldom become lovers in anything more than the physical sense. The sexual predicament of the G.I.s is more acute and unhappy in Vietnam than in almost any theatre where the United States has its forces.

The French in colonial days used to maintain one enormous brothel in Cholon for the benefit of the troops. A visit to this establishment is described in a memorable scene of Graham Greene's *The Quiet American*. When the Diem government closed houses of prostitution, the girls began to operate in the bars of the entertainment quarters of Saigon but particularly in the downtown Tu Do district, near to the west bank of the river. The old-timers deplore the fact that so many soldiers now roam the city centre. The French, they point out, never allowed this. There is even a plan to construct a special red-light district which the police can control and which the girls will not be allowed to leave. Meanwhile the lonely soldier enjoys neither the certain merchandise of the brothel nor the consolations of quiet drinking.

A night out in Saigon is a gloomy occasion. Unless the G.I. visits one of the service clubs he is likely to pass most of his time in a bar, because the movies are in French and the night-clubs offer appalling shows with Korean female impersonators and stars of Philippine T.V. quiz programmes. Having found a seat in the bar, the G.I. will buy a can of American beer for six shillings or, if he is feeling poor, a bottle of Vietnamese beer for three shillings. By the time his drink has been poured, a girl will have sat down beside him. She will be wearing a Western dress and a permanent wave and a big, false bosom, because this is the style of beauty the G.I.s prefer. She would look very much prettier with her hair trailing low over the slit-sided *ao dai* and pantaloons of traditional Vietnam. (It is curious to observe that the *ao dai* is not only disapproved of but actually banned in Communist North Vietnam.) The bar girl will say to the G.I.: 'What's your name? You number one! Sorry about that! No kidding! You very handsome!' for these are the only phrases of English she knows. He will buy her a glass of Saigon Tea for six shillings. Years ago the bar girls used to pretend that this drink was really whisky instead of cold tea, but now it is recognized as a ticket to purchase the girl's company at the bar during the next half-hour. The G.I. will talk to her about his wife, girl, mother, job, studies, motor car or favourite football team. She will stare over his shoulder and say: 'You number one! No kidding!' and so on. Every now and then she will give him a playful, reproving slap on the assumption that he has made some suggestive remark. Even if he is telling her that his buddies have all been killed in a mortar attack and his mother is dying of cancer, she will still slap his arm and say: 'You very handsome! You number one!' Sometimes she will play him at gin rummy or pontoon. She is sober and good at cards and will take some money off him. She does not smoke or drink alcohol but she will eat snacks throughout the evening: rice and *noc mam* sauce, oranges, peanuts, ham sandwiches, crab meat and duck eggs. He will continue to drink beer and to offer her one Saigon Tea every half-hour until eleven o'clock which is closing time because of the coming curfew. If the bar is disreputable, he may go back to the girl's room where he stands a twenty-five per cent chance of getting V.D. and a five per cent chance of getting robbed.

One bar girl who was friendly and spoke some French described how she went about her work. 'I like this bar because it is quiet without many girls. And I only have to be here from five in the evening till ten-thirty. I have a maid to do the housework so I can spend most of the day doing what I like best which is sleeping. I spend eight shillings a day on taxis going to and from work and I would buy a Honda except that I live on the third floor and therefore have nowhere to park it. When I get back at night I read the newspapers until about three in the morning, then sleep, wake up for breakfast, go back to sleep again, then maybe go to a movie or visit a friend before coming to work in the bar.' She is a rather cynical girl with a laugh on a falling series of notes, like some tropical bird. Her girl friends say, and she half admits, that she is fairly promiscuous, but she does not go to bed with the Americans who provide her income in Saigon Tea. The pretty, amusing bar girls earn so much money from chaste work that they do not need to supplement it by prostitution.

The Americans who were stationed in Japan after the Second World War became very fond of Japanese girls. I have read several novels and seen as many American films about G.I.s who wanted to marry their little Cio-Cio-Sans but were barred from doing so by a tyrannous army. Many American novels contrast the affectionate, graceful and feminine Japanese girls with their neurotic, aggressive and frigid American counterparts. There have been just as eloquent books extolling the girls of Hong Kong, the Philippines and Thailand. So far there has been no such legend concerning the girls of Vietnam although these are the most attractive in Asia. Many Americans speak with ill feeling about the Vietnamese girls. Shortly after Senator Fulbright accused his fellow-countrymen of having 'turned Saigon into a brothel' an American sergeant remarked to me: 'We haven't turned it into a brothel. It's just that the girls now are taking money for what they used to do free.' Of course this is not true at all. There have always been prostitutes in Vietnam. There have always been girls who would not be seen with a foreigner. The Americans who say that Vietnamese girls are hard and mercenary cannot have understood the local customs. Any Vietnamese girl who wants to get married will expect her husband to pay a large money gift to her parents. In the same way she will feel obliged to be paid for becoming a temporary wife or mistress. Many an American has set up house with a Vietnamese girl. He pays the rent and the food and on top of this makes her a monthly payment of a hundred dollars. Yet the same American may feel shocked by this mercenary arrangement, which offends his sense of romance and sentiment.

The American cannot imagine love that is paid for. The Vietnamese would be shocked by the girl who went to live with a man out of love alone, and without taking money to give to her family. One hears of cases in Vietnam where a U.S. serviceman, after a long relationship with a paid mistress, has tried to throw her out of the house by stopping her monthly pay. The girl has protested her love and begged to be kept on even without pay. The Americans cannot understand that Vietnamese women are both mercenary and romantic. The very mercenary instinct is part of a pious sense of family duty. I have known one or two girls 'of good family' who talk about going to work in a bar just as a Spanish girl would talk of joining a convent. It is the ultimate sacrifice in the family name. However, this sense of duty is also mixed with a sense of romance and curiosity, for Vietnamese girls, behind their apparent hardness and business sense, have a very romantic attitude to Americans. This unexpected attitude became clear to me after long conversations with various girls and from a study of Vietnamese novels and magazine serials.

One Vietnamese girl who has lived abroad said that American men were far more kind and considerate than the Vietnamese. Moreover, simple girls who had learned their ideas of love from the cinema were astonished to meet Americans who looked like Gregory Peck and Marlon Brando. She also affirmed, though without much amplification, that Americans were better lovers physically than the Vietnamese. The typical serial in a women's pulp magazine describes a Vietnamese girl in love with a young criminal or delinquent. In order to bail him out of prison she has to take a job in a bar where she meets an older American who is rich and kind and eventually marries her—in the sense of taking her as a paid mistress. My friend says that Americans would be even better portrayed in these serials were it not for the fact that the authors were men.

These stories have taken the theme of Madam Butterfly but managed to turn it inside out. The American has become the loving and trusting victim, the girl is the hard exploiter. The realism of Asians is matched against American sentimentality and puritanism. One typical newspaper serial tells of an American captain who wants to meet a girl-friend in Saigon. A middle-aged procuress takes him to a bar and introduces him to a girl 'of good family'. She tells him that she is interested only in money. He says that he wants to marry her because she is a virgin. Finally she overcomes his scruples and they arrange to set up house on a paying basis. On the first night together she is quite calm and composed because, although she is still a virgin, she knows she has made her break with the past. He on the other hand is overcome by his puritanical conscience which makes him nervous and, by implication, impotent. Before they can consummate their liaison a bomb falls on the house and kills them both.

The popular folk-stories and novels of Vietnam, like the Chinese tales from which they derive, often recount the agony of a girl who has to decide between her love for a poor man and her duty towards the family. This duty often obliges her to marry an older but rich man whom she cannot learn to love. This ancient theme is sometimes adapted to life in South Vietnam, where a girl is obliged to find herself an American. This theme appears in the recent novel *War* by the Saigon author Chu Tu, who is also a practising psychologist. Since the book has not been translated from Vietnamese, I asked a friend to give me this summary of the plot and the argument.

The heroine Dao is a southern girl who has gone to a French school and whose modern ideas disagree with those of her very conservative parents. She falls in love with Hiep, an idealistic refugee from the north, who is in turn in love with another girl, Huyen. In the confused politics of the time, which is during the Diem regime, Huyen is tortured and raped by pirates, while Dao has to marry a Communist in order to save her family. Both girls now feel disgraced. After the death of the Communist villain, Dao 'in her complete despair' meets a former girl-friend married to an American. The friend advises her to do the same. 'A foreign husband will not investigate your past like a Vietnamese would. He has a lot of money, he knows how to please his wife, how to love. And when you are tired of each other, you can always live peacefully. When one's past is not so pure, it is disastrous to marry a man of the same country.'

Dao asks her friend to find an American—and Casey appears. Big, handsome and moustached, Casey is fascinated by the delicate, beautiful girl with her fatalistic and *risquée* air. He 'blushes like a little child' (a feature of Westerners that intrigues the Vietnamese) and, being intelligent, knows that Dao is not really in love with him. 'I'm sad because your voice reveals that you are not in love yet and I don't want an affair without love. And I don't believe that the Vietnamese are only in love with money. You are an irresistible woman and I will make you love me,' he says. Dao reminds herself that 'I only want to marry a foreigner for money but he is not stupid and I'm afraid I might fall in love with him. However, I will despise myself if I love a foreigner.' But when Casey kisses her she realizes that she is not in love with him or Hiep or any man—but only with herself. Another girl-friend tells Dao: 'I have had many foreign lovers and I have found out that I have never loved any of them sincerely; whether the foreigner loves me truthfully or not, I never know. We are Vietnamese to our very bones and our very soul. Maybe we can love a foreigner but that is not the same kind of feeling we have for a Vietnamese.'

At the end of the novel Dao gets a letter from Hiep who is in exile in Cambodia. Telling Casey that she must make a business trip, she goes to join Hiep for a last moment of happiness after which she will take her own life. So the novel ends in a classical Vietnamese tragedy. But the author Chu Tu, who is more than a trifle cynical, has added a second, alternative ending in the form of an epilogue years later. Dao has married the engineer and lives with him in a big villa on Nguyen Du Street. Hiep, who has lost all his ideals, now teaches at a private school in another part of Saigon. He sees Dao only to borrow her P.X. card for a bottle of whisky 'to get drunk and forget about life'.

IF YOU FLY TO SAIGON FROM BANGKOK OR SINGAPORE, YOU GET YOUR first impressions of Vietnam from the Delta that forms the south-west tip of the country. Seen from a high-flying jet plane, this countryside is not attractive. It is of course very flat but also unexpectedly colour-less. The green looks grey; the red mud turns to a pale brown. The mighty Mekong and Bassac rivers, and all the hundreds of streams and canals that serve them, look at this height like the trails of crustaceans and worms on some oily and evil-smelling sea shore. This had been my first thought when I looked down at the Delta on coming in from Bangkok and I remember the shock I had when the American next to me in the plane said: 'This place could be a tourist paradise except for the war.' But he was right.

My first trip to the Delta was made in a small propeller-powered plane that flew only a few thousand feet above the ground. From this height the countryside looked far more attractive. I could see the shimmering green of the paddy fields and the red of the flooded rivers carrying rich soil from Cambodia, Laos and China. I could pick out the houses along the river bank, the small hamlets crouched by their bamboo fences, the junks and skiffs making their way through the criss-cross maze of the water traffic system. I also noticed the many immense pockmarks left on the land by the bombs and shells. For reasons which must be explained, the Delta has always been a major theatre of the war.

The peasants of the Delta make up half the population of South Vietnam and they provide the distinctive southern character which is so often held up to contrast with that of the northerners. They are placid, easy going, a little lazy and rather pious. The northerners are by contrast dour, fanatic and radical. This difference is often advanced as a reason why South and North Vietnam should be kept apart and ruled by the two systems of politics for which they are suited by temperament. It is a theory that does not stand up to argument. The most anti-Communist people in South Vietnam are refugees from the North, the bourgeoisie of Saigon and the other big cities, and certain religious sects. The Delta has always been a stronghold of Communist feeling. The government holds the main towns but most of the countryside is, in American parlance, insecure.

Why should a district so rich be so sympathetic to Communism? The waters teem with fish, crabs, frogs, snakes and other Vietnamese delicacies. Their floods nourish the rice paddies. They provide drink, cleanliness, and somewhere to get cool from the sun. Even in French times, Cochin China was always considered the most placid and prosperous area of the country and its exports of rice went to most of the Far East. However, the peasants themselves did not get a fair share of the wealth of the river. Great landlords appropriated half or more of the annual rice crop and often forced the peasants into debt with the merchants, Even today, as I saw and shall describe, the peasants have scarcely gained from the much vaunted programmes of land reform. The Japanese, and later the Vietminh, encouraged the Delta peasants to claim the land for themselves and by 1954 this was a revolutionary stronghold. The Communist dominance in the Delta was a source of great economic advantage as well as political power, since whoever controlled it also controlled the sale of rice.

I made several trips to the Delta, visiting certain towns and districts two or three times. I begin with My Tho, which is near to Saigon; then Can Tho, the largest town; quiet Long Xuyen; and lastly the island of Phu Quoc, which lies west of the mainland of South Vietnam.

*   *   *

Highway Four from Saigon to My Tho remined me of the A4 from London to Slough. It passes through miles of dirty, ramshackle suburbs; it is fringed with small factories; and it might, if peace arrived, become a major industrial area. The countryside is dull and disordered and the traffic is dangerous. The heavy lorries, both civil and military, ride on the crown of the road. Smaller cars and innumerable motor-cycles fight for space between the road and the ditch. Long queues form at the bridges, which are guarded by dust-stained tanks. The Vietcong sometimes manage to plant a bomb on Highway Four in the hope of setting it off under a truckload of troops, but the traffic is more of a danger. On any trip you are likely to see at least one bus on its back—like a dead dog—in the paddy field beside the road.

The open road to Saigon has made My Tho a very prosperous city. The government, understanding this, deploys a major part of its troops in the Delta to guarding Highway Four and the other lines of communication. The American A.I.D. officials, who want to encourage subsidiary crops to break the peasants' dependence on rice, have seen the road as a way of encouraging market gardens. 'We're encouraging vegetables,' said an A.I.D. official in My Tho, 'because people who are growing vegetables and making money on their produce are not going to want to pay off guerillas. Another reason they're growing a lot of vegetables is that the V.C. are shooting water buffalo and you can grow vegetables without buffalo.' In private, Americans will admit to a third reason: the peasants can grow vegetables without paying such a heavy rent as they do on rice.

The U.S. agricultural adviser in My Tho, Captain Hardy Graves, took me to see the allotments alongside Highway Four. We talked to an onion farmer who nets ten thousand piastres a year from a patch only a hundred metres by ten metres. Another farmer had planted water melons on one acre of land and earned three hundred thousand piastres on an investment of thirty thousand. Water melons fetch their highest price at Tet, the New Year Festival, when they are used as special offerings on the family altar. A very big melon may sell for eight hundred piastres in My Tho, or fifteen hundred in Saigon; newcomers, who think of South Vietnam as a poor country, are startled to hear that people will pay five pounds for a water melon.

The business has done so well near My Tho that the town was holding its first-ever contest for water melons. Three serious men from the Ministry of Agriculture had driven down from Saigon to grace the occasion; beaming Americans tasted slices of melon and praised its sweetness; the shy peasant competitors, with their hair done up in braids, stood round the side of the room and puffed cigarettes and ate dishes of green jelly. Afterwards Captain Graves was angry because the officials from Saigon had taken the surplus melons away in their car. 'You know how the farmers think about the government. Well, how are they going to think about that when they know that the price is going to be twice as high in Saigon? The melons should have been given away.'

Like many agricultural officers, Captain Graves is an Army man who was drafted into this para-civilian duty. 'He was chosen by I.B.M.' said an admiring colleague, 'and if the computer works that well, then everyone should be chosen by I.B.M. The last man we had was a missile expert but the machine picked up that he'd graduated in agriculture in Texas.' Captain Graves is also a southerner and he says that the Mekong and Mississippi Deltas are much alike. Both have superb soil, a sleepy charm, and enormous political problems. One afternoon we drove farther along Highway Four, to the outer extent of the vegetable plots. It was very hot and the crimson dragon-flies seemed to be half asleep on the wing. The water had drained out of the paddy fields, leaving a rim of rich mud in which the local children were fishing by hand. One little toddler was naked and covered from head to toe in layers of various-coloured clay, like a bushman dressed for a ceremony. He was strangling a large fish in chubby hands while a girl rubbed dollops of mud into his pate. We asked the children to show us their home and they led the way along a series of earth dykes through the paddy fields.

The head of the family was a lean, sardonic man in his sixties who had moved here recently from a more dangerous area. He was not yet a vegetable farmer but there was evidence all over the cottage that he did a big business in making straw hats. He brought out a teapot and filled our cups, to the great delight of Captain Graves, who seemed to take an almost proprietorial pride in the courtesy of the local peasants. We asked our host about his land and he said he rented the paddy field which he had just crossed. It normally yielded seventy *gias* of paddy rice of which he gave twenty-five as rent to the landlord. However, last year's floods had been so bad that the actual yield was only twenty-five *gias*. We accepted a second cup of tea and asked the farmer how much rent he would have to pay this year, in view of the bad harvest. The farmer replied that he and the other tenants near by would refuse to pay any rent at all. If the landlord insisted 'many farmers will want to go to the V.C.' We understood this remark as a joke and asked the farmer to tell us about his family. He said that one son was in prison for having refused to join the army. The interview seemed to be going badly and Captain Graves asked if the farmer 'had faith in the government.' The interpreter posed the question, listened to the reply, and said: 'No.' Although Captain Graves was rather taken aback he decided to make a joke of the issue and asked if the farmer had faith in the Vietcong. Again the interpreter talked and listened. This time the answer was 'Yes.' The captain put down his cup in dismay. 'I wish we hadn't taken more tea,' he said, 'because now we've got to go without drinking it.' Before we went, the farmer gave us a few more comments on agriculture in South Vietnam 'where the rich get richer and the poor get poorer.' He was very bitter or very brave to state such views in such company.

The province of Dinh Tuong, like Gaul, is divided into three parts. The government and the Vietcong each control a third of the geo-graphical area and the remainder is still 'contested'. However, the government third contains My Tho itself and the other population centres. The Vietcong are strongest in the desolate northern sector adjoining the Plain of Reeds. The American Province Representative said that with twenty per cent more troops they could achieve one hundred and fifty per cent more pacification. Meanwhile they were winning over the peasants in districts already controlled. He had a map of the province showing the 626 hamlets in the area of which 549 had still to be pacified. One of the main weapons of pacification here is the ten 'cadre teams', trained and financed by the U.S. Government in its 'revolutionary development' programme. The fifty-nine men in each team have all done a three-month course at Vung Tau on the coast and are meant to live like the villagers, even wearing the humble costume of black pyjamas. The black pyjamas, the words like 'cadre' and 'revolution', have echoes of just that Communism that 'cadre teams' are intended to fight. The likeness is quite intentional. The Americans, just like the French and Diem before them, much admire the techniques of their enemy. They cannot admit to themselves that Communist ideology is a source of strength; therefore the Communists must have achieved power by technique. Therefore the same technique, sup-ported by true ideology, will defeat the Communist uprising. This policy did not help the French nor Diem, for reasons that now lie in history. Some Americans doubt the utility of the present R.D. (Revo-lutionary Development) cadres. The teams are seldom villagers, but usually middle class boys from the town. Their selection depends on the Vietnamese Province Chief who may use this power to reward political friends or exact bribes. Many are outright loafers, with long manicured fingernails and sloppy clothes.

86

The cadre team I saw at Than Dao, near My Tho, looked rather smarter than the average. Most of the team were present although it was near to the Tet holiday. Most were wearing their black uniforms. Most of their guns were clean. They had been in the hamlet only three weeks and did not claim to have made much impression. 'There are many V.C. sympathizers in the village,' said Nguyen Van Tung, the detachment leader. 'Almost all the population have relatives with the V.C. The young men between twenty-one and thirty are frightened of going into the Vietnamese army and they have gone to a V.C.-controlled hamlet.' In fact I saw almost no civilian males between the ages of fifteen and fifty. Only the village idiot walked through the dust to salute the visitors from the government with a slobbering murmur and tight handclasp just as, no doubt, he had recently greeted the Vietcong.

'Contact with Charlie has been negative,' said the Vietnamese guide, meaning that Vietcong and cadres had not yet met in battle. However, the cadres were busy with Civic Action work like repairing walls and roofs. And 'every night from ten to twelve they have a motivation team singing songs to the V.C.' Songs, music and dance are some of the cadres' special weapons. Today a team of musicians had come from Saigon to give one of the propaganda concerts. Their stars were a man in rimless glasses and a quite pretty girl with bangs. Most of them carried guitars and had once worked with civilian groups such as the Spotlights and the Vampires. Their present job was part of their national service. The man in rimless glasses stopped under the largest tree in the village, brought his guitar to the ready and beckoned the children to gather round. 'Now I'm going to sing you a song', he began, 'about Vietnam: "Vietnam! Vietnam! The word I heard when I was born." Just sing this song when Charlie comes to the village and he'll run away. There'll be some candy for the children who sing it best.' He sang the first lines over and over again until a few of the quicker children were singing it with him. Then he taught them the chorus with a lilting melody rather like 'Loch Lomond': 'Vietnam! Vietnam! The sound of a child rocking in its cradle.' The words puzzled me. 'Vietnam' is quite unlike the sound of a child rocking in its cradle. It sounds more like a rusty gate.

Under the neighbouring tree, the girl with bangs had gathered together a smaller audience of the womenfolk. She sang 'about women who feel sorry that their men have gone away and are calling

Farmers and Cadres in the Delta

them to come back.' It was a mournful tune whose effect was a little spoiled by various twangs and pings from the loud-speaker. The village women listened in silence.

While the women and children listened to songs, the cadres and the Popular Force soldiers had gathered outside the hamlet to watch a series of cock-fights. The owners and their birds came from villages round about and some from as far as My Tho. About forty people were here to bet and to watch the contest within a small circle of ropes. The referee lit a joss stick, the owners pointed the cocks face to face and soon the battle was bloody. The start of the match is always tense because if one of the birds runs away before the joss stick has burned three inches, the match is void and the bets are cancelled. Even afterwards there are many pauses and intervals to revive the battered cocks. After a sharp clash, the owner picks up the bird and sucks the comb on its head and blows water under its wings.

After about ten minutes the fight is stopped to allow for major repairs. The owner sews up the cuts with a needle and thread. He shoves a feather down the bird's throat to sop up the blood. He puts the whole head in his mouth and spits out a great gout of blood to the merriment of the audience. Soon after the fight has resumed the birds reopen the stitched wounds and soon blood dribbles all over the tiny arena. They are too tired to jump in the air but instead peck at each other's eyes and burrow under each other's wings. The audience gets very excited. One man tried to assault one of the owners. 'He says that man kicked his chicken,' the cadre explained. 'He says he cheats. So he gets pissed off.' The white cock, which had been favourite, has cuts all over its head like the British heavyweight Henry Cooper. Blind and choking, it stumbles round the ring while a girl spectator screams with delight—just as Tolstoy's Natasha screams when she sees the kill of the she-wolf. The white cock suddenly falls and lies on its side and gasps. A member of the cadre looks at the raw, bleeding neck and laughs with real pleasure. Those who have bet on the other cock gather round to jeer at the white bird's owner who walks off in a state near to tears. The cadre member whispers to me: 'In the morning the chickens fight. In the evening the people fight.' The sport is well suited to Vietnam. It appeals to the two national passions for bloodshed and gambling.

After the cock-fights I went to the old Buddhist temple at Thanh Phu which had just been recovered from V.C. control. The Americans were repairing the temple as part of their Civic Action work and had mounted a floodlight behind one of the statues of the Buddha. Inside the temple, nothing seemed to have changed. The inner courtyard was filled with tall jars and purple flowers. Golden painted Buddhas smiled from the dark walls. There were many statues of cranes standing on tortoises. A nun showed us the old bell in which the Emperor Gia Long was supposed to have hidden from enemies during a whole night. The bell was about three feet tall and only two feet in diameter but the nun, at any rate, seemed to believe the story. Recent history has not affected the convent. The nun said she was pleased that tourists could once more come to visit the convent, which boasts a brand new calender showing a housewife jumping for joy because she has bought a gas cooker. 'Had the Vietcong misbehaved?' I asked the nun through the cadre interpreter. 'Negative, sir,' the answer came. 'She says Charlie never bothered them.'

*   *   *

I have lodged in various quarters in Can Tho but the worst was the large and rambling bawdy house that its owners call a hotel. The bed was a wooden board; the neighbours were noisy; and whatever I asked for, from tea to an early call, the porter would send up instead one of the pock-marked and no doubt pox-ridden prostitutes. Can Tho is a dirty and sullen town with a reputation for graft and bad government. The Vietcong do not trouble it much, either because, as some think, the population is anti-Communist; or because, as others think, there are so many Communists that any attack would kill more of them than of us.

Can Tho, like Manchester, is a city you spend most of your time trying to get out of. On the first occasion I went on foot with a small group of Australian engineers. It had been planned to go for a boat trip on the Bassac and we assembled the necessary gear of a rifle, a fishing-rod, cameras and several cans of lager. We hailed some cyclos and headed for what I imagined would be the jetty. However, it turned out that the boat was moored to a dredge and that to reach the dredge we had to walk along a length of pipe. I did not comprehend this at the time.

The pipeline led from the dredge across thirty yards of the Bassac, across an island of paddy fields, across another arm of the Bassac, and then across a number of fields to the airport where the sand from the dredge would be used. As soon as we arrived at the airport and I realized that I would have to walk along this pipe I felt an intense unease. I have no sense of balance and even although the pipe was twelve inches across, the actual surface on which one could tread was only six inches wide. For the first few hundred yards the pipe led over a muddy field and was scarcely raised from the ground. When we came to the bank of the first river I thought we had come to the end and looked round for the boat. When one of the Australians explained that we were to cross along the drain-pipe—raised ten or twelve feet over the stream—I thought that he must be joking. But we climbed the steps and started to walk across. For the first few yards there was a piece of cable at waist height which served as a balancer but after that one was obliged to rely on balance alone. As soon as we had crossed the bridge we set off to cross the island on a pipe once again raised high above the ground. This journey to me was torment. My legs shook. I swayed. When I stopped I felt dizzy. If I walked too fast my legs seemed to sway too far out on either side of the pipe. The sun was broiling hot and sweat streamed over my spectacles. At the sound of small-arms fire in the middle distance I found myself hoping that it would come near, therefore giving us all a chance to dive for cover into the paddy field. When we finally reached the dredge and the motor boat, they told me that we had walked a mile and a half along the drain. It was a forceful introduction to the problem of land trans-port in the Delta where many Vietnamese traverse the paddies along thin bamboo poles.

Once on the dredge I mounted the fishing-rod, baited the hook with some prawns and started to fish in the river. However, the water was so deep and the current so powerful in this flood season that I could not settle the bait on the river bottom, even when using a large steel bolt as a sinker. The Vietnamese guards advised me to go back to the island and fish in the pools. I took this advice, although it meant walking back fifty yards on the dreaded drain-pipe, and soon had taken up position on a strip of bank dividing two ponds. The peasants use these ponds to raise fish and to grow water lilies whose nuts are called 'buffalo horns' because of their shape. These nuts are about an inch and a half long, very white inside, and crisp and refreshing to taste.

Looking up from my fishing I saw that a tiny reed skiff had drawn near, manned by a boy and a girl of about twelve or fourteen. The girl, in the usual conical hat, was very shy but they both picked me buffalo horns and threw them on to the bank beside me. Their handsome, friendly faces, the gracefulness of the skiff on the pond and the lush green of the paddy fields stretching away from me combined to produce a wonderful feeling of quiet. Several fish had snatched at my bait and jiggled the improvised float I had made from a chunk of wood, but their mouths were no doubt too small for the large sea-fishing hook I had borrowed. Suddenly, in a moment of high farce, a large catfish jumped clean out of the pond and fell on to the bank some thirty yards from where I sat. It was immediately captured and killed by some other children who demonstrated to me, with much mocking sign language, that I could not even catch fish that were bent on suicide. Then a slightly older boy asked me to give him a cigarette, which I had to refuse for I do not smoke. He scowled, tapped his chest and said 'V.C.', at which all the other children drifted away. A machine-gun opened up somewhere quite close and I remembered that this island was thought to be 'insecure'. The fish showed no sign of hooking themselves and the clouds were building up to a storm so I walked back along the drain-pipe to the dredge. No sooner was I aboard than the light diminished almost to dusk and the storm broke with stupendous fury. The river had darkened into a deep chocolate brown, the mangroves on the opposite shore were black, and the junks that passed us going down-stream were shadows in the darkness. Then the rain ceased, the sun reappeared, and the landscape of the Bassac was once again as peaceful and fresh as the Norfolk Broads.

Late that night I returned to the river, where the breeze was as cool and as soft as a silk scarf. The crickets were trilling all around but the peace of the night was broken by sounds of the war. On the other side of the river the Americans were carrying out the operation called 'Puff from the Magic Dragon'. The quaint and facetious title belies the murderous fact. An old C-47 plane, fitted with six machine-guns, circles slowly over an area which is believed to contain Vietcong. Brilliant flares are dropped to illuminate the target and as the plane flies round it pounds the ground at the intensity of one bullet per square foot. Every fifth bullet is red tracer so that one sees the flow of bullets curving slowly into the target like a stream of diseased urine.

I was watching this performance from a boat moored to the Can Tho shore. Next to me was an ARVIN soldier who watched the river. He seemed to be paying attention to the clumps of weed and tree that floated down stream, for whenever one of these stopped in its course at the sides of the boat or under the jetty he fired a shot or a burst into the weed. The Vietcong like to swim under the protection of the weed in order to stick limpet mines on government targets.

In the evenings we drank beer in the Can Tho Club or the villas of various Americans and Australians. The young Australian dredging engineer, Mike Carthy, used to go out at night with his six-foot-long tame python, named Saigon Tea. He bought the creature at a market for three pounds, or rather more than the price it was going to fetch as meat; but it more than paid for itself as entertainment. Saigon Tea sleeps most of the day but he comes to life when there is company and slithers from chair to chair running his long, flickering tongue over the guests and sometimes coiling himself round a leg or a shoulder. A Vietnamese girl lives in one of the villas where Saigon Tea is taken to drink. As soon as she sees the snake she locks herself in the back room and will open it only so far as to slip through a few cans of beer from the ice-box. This timidity amuses her boy-friend who says that at first she was even afraid at coming to live in such a big house because she thought there were ghosts. Moreover, the Indian films she saw were full of ghosts and magic in which the evil genie appears as a snake. Carthy says that the Vietnamese cannot distinguish between the dangerous and the harmless snakes. They will kill a harmless python and allow themselves to be bitten by small poisonous snakes. Once he took Saigon Tea into the Can Tho Club in a basket and the Indian doorman looked inside to see if he was smuggling whisky. It was so dark, so Carthy recalls, that the Indian put his head almost into the basket before he discerned the python. Unfortunately the python did not scare the bar girls, who petted it and charged many drinks for doing so. 'I gave him a sip of Saigon Tea,' Carthy remarked, 'and he recoiled in horror. That's how he got his name. But he likes beer. If you feed him beer, he's your friend.'

Many foreigners in Vietnam have made friends with exotic pets. One evening in Can Tho I went to the Special Forces Mess called the Alamo Club where the 'men in the green berets' were drinking and talking against the unceasing noise from the juke box of the 'Song of the Green Beret'. After the usual talk about who had got clap that week and which of the 'slope' girls had 'gotten knocked up', the conversation came round again to pets. A sergeant said: 'We used to keep a snake out there and a monkey. Jesus, that monkey was horny. He'd screw everything that moved except the snake. The secretaries were terrified of him. He'd come into the room and take a leap at them with his prick stuck out in front like a ramrod.' Many G.I.s also keep cats.

Over the bar at the Alamo Club there hangs an oil painting about eight feet by four feet of a girl lying face down on a settee wearing only an unbuttoned shirt. She is reaching out to adjust the record player and one of her legs hangs over the side of the settee. A glass of wine is on the floor beside her and a green beret hangs on the wall in the corner. I was told that a Chinese girl in Can Tho does these paintings from photographs in *Playboy* and kindred magazines, adding details such as the green beret by request. I went to see the artist, Miss Le Nguyet Hang, who is twenty-two and lives and works at a small studio near to my lodgings. She told me that she came from a family of artists in Long Xuyen, a few miles to the north, and she had wanted to start up on her own after three years of art school in Saigon. She told me that she earned her living mostly by doing paintings from photographs, for which she charged between seven and thirty-five pounds. She does about four of these a week. She also does the occasional painting for clubs, such as the one I had seen at the Special Forces Mess. The most important Commissions from the Americans are for paintings of wives or families done from the photographs that they carry around in their wallets. One could see the result of her work on the walls. There was a Negro boy in tartan jacket smiling toothily into the camera. There was an old couple, doggedly side by side, like a *Time* Magazine cover to illustrate the American Heritage.

Miss Le, like all artists who happen to have a commercial success, talked wistfully of the real paintings she wanted to do if she only had more time. In the evenings, she says, she does landscapes and portraits from life, but all of the day is spent on working from photographs. She seemed amused rather than shocked by the *Playboy* pictures but I should like to have found out what she really thought of these huge, bare girls with pouting lips and breasts and behinds. Miss Le herself is a subtle and dainty creature. I asked her what sort of paintings the Vietnamese soldiers bought. They couldn't afford them, she said. But what would they buy if they could afford them? Miss Le thought for a moment and said they would buy landscapes with the family appearing in them. And sometimes, she thought, they would buy the *Playboy* pictures, but only to hang in the bedroom—not in the living-room.

There are half a dozen galleries in Tu Do in Saigon offering pastel scenes of tigers up a tree, sampans gliding in the moonlight, or medieval warlords with curving swords. Some Americans buy this muck and more Vietnamese would buy if only they had the money. Occasionally there are exhibitions by good local painters who manage to sell a canvas or two at fifty dollars. These might be pleasant fantasies, echoing Modigliani, Chagall and Buffet; collages of lacquered paper from *Life* and *Paris Match*; or a few wistful essays on life in the Vietnamese countryside. The elegant and romantic tradition of Vietnam can be found in most of these paintings—but seldom a hint of the war. I did see the work of one artist in which the traditional masked gods of war were juxtaposed with carbines and howitzers of the present-day conflict, but the shape of these hard metal objects on bare canvas reminded me more of the abstracts of Leger than of real life in Vietnam.

To see the war transformed into art one has only to look at the statue in front of the parliament building in Saigon. This gross and obscene portrayal of two soldiers was mounted in 1966 to mark the Republic's National Day. A company of the Ranger troops constructed and may have designed this work. They built a substructure of metal rods, then chucked on cement with trowels, then slapped on a second layer to give the figure a rugged appearance, then finally sprayed the whole thing with gold paint to give an impression of worn bronze. The people of Saigon still wince at the outcome, which portrays two soldiers advancing in crouch position with guns poised and backsides grotesquely bulging. The one behind is urging his comrade forward by tapping him with a carbine butt, and of course the statue has bred a number of crude jokes. The soldiers are sodomites, or baboons, or a launching a military coup against the parliament. The Vietnamese say it represents the American soldier taking cover behind the Vietnamese. The Americans say the reverse. More serious people sigh over the misery of a country that can throw up such art.

* * *

An American information officer in Can Tho said that the Vietcong in the Delta were desperate—so desperate that they had started to mortar provincial capitals. 'We're going to get it in Can Tho soon. There's nothing to stop them. This is a sign of defeat for the V.C. All their idealists have now gone. All that are left are a few people who've spent their lives in the movement and have to go on living for it because they can't face up to the murders they have committed.' He thought that the military victory had nearly been won by now but political victory was not yet won. 'The mass of the peasants are still not excited about the government. They still won't denounce the V.C. But anybody who thinks the people still like the V.C. is deluding himself. We emphasize in our propaganda that the V.C. are fighting against *people*.' This is how things seemed to the information officer in Can Tho. They seemed different to me at the nearby village of Co Do, where I spent the next few days.

Like many parts of the Delta, the district round Co Do is said to be one-third controlled by the government, one-third controlled by the V.C., and one-third contested between the two. As elsewhere, the mass of the population live in the towns or villages which are controlled by the government. The government forces and their American helpers base themselves in the largest town or village and try to extend their influence in a circle outwards to where the V.C. live in remote huts or on sampans. Normally the size of the circle corresponds to the maximum range of the howitzers at the district headquarters. These keep up a harassing fire on the V.C. who therefore try to establish their bases out of howitzer range.

The political geography of the Delta can be described with beermats on a bar. The mats correspond to the circles of government strength while the V.C. live in the gaps in between. The government has not yet been able to cover the whole Delta with howitzer fire and the gaps have to be dealt with by air attacks. Many are 'free strike' or 'select strike' zones, meaning that aeroplanes can use bombs, napalm or machine-gun fire against any movement within those areas. In theory the Vietnamese Province Chief must give permission for every air strike. In theory these Province Chiefs take great pains to make sure that no attacks are made on harmless civilians. In practice both Vietnamese and Americans tend to regard these 'select strike zones' as justifiable targets. I asked one American who had just ordered a strike on some huts and some sampans (blowing the latter to bits 'with parts of the boat and bodies flying in all directions') if air attacks like this did not kill many harmless civilians. 'But people shouldn't continue to live there,' he said. The result has been to drive the population inwards towards the towns and large villages. The U.S. adviser at Co Do, Major Ned Digh, said he had recently done a survey of refugees 'and couldn't find any refugees from the V.C. With one man it might mean that there'd been an air strike. With the others it was just that the grass looked greener across the way.'

From Co Do you can see miles in every direction across the enormous chequer board of the paddy fields. In the distance, out on the edge of the circle of fire, one can generally see the smoke of some air attack or artillery fire. The radio in the Company H.Q. chatters with constant news from the ground control and the spotter pilots. One morning everyone grew excited because a pilot reported having seen ten freshly dug graves. The lieutenant explained to me that this presaged a battle within the district: 'The V.C. dig the graves before they go on an operation. They tell the men that ten or twelve of them aren't going to come back. Sometimes they even hold a formal service for them beforehand.'

Most of the rice land around Co Do had once belonged to a big French company. The present district chief and his American advisers live in the tall, gabled houses that once belonged to the plantation agents. The Americans say that the last French agent here had been murdered by the villagers because of the company's tyranny. Nothing of France remains except for the houses—in silly mimicry of a Loire chateau—and a rusting steamroller beside the canal. The Saigon government has taken over the French land and offered it to the peasants for rent or sale. On paper, the government has bought out the big Vietnamese landowners as part of its land reform programme. I questioned many peasants about their rent and their tax but seldom received any clear answer. Some said that they still paid rent to the landlords who had been expropriated. Almost all of them paid sacks of rice to the district chief but were uncertain if this was rent or tax.

The district chief is a dapper ARVIN captain and therefore a rank below his adviser Major Digh, but the two men work together with wry good humour. The captain lives in awe of his wife, who comes from a rich family in My Tho, and she accompanies him on his Jeep trips, dressed in a fetching camouflage suit, with a smart perm and lavishly painted finger and toe nails. A big dog sniffs and drools at her heels as she does her 'social work' of chatting to peasant women about their babies and cooking. The peasants regard her with gawping reserve. She reminded me of those pictures you see in *Country Life* showing Lord So-and-so's beautiful wife making friends with his crofters in the north of Scotland.

The junior ARVIN officers have had to leave their wives at home and they do not mix with the local girls. In their Officers' Mess, so the U.S. lieutenant recounted, they generally dance with each other. 'They wanted me to give them dancing lessons but, goddam it, it's bad enough their being so short but they also want to lead.' The Americans have refused this form of aid and advice.

The four U.S. advisers at Co Do are quite exceptionally pleasant and intelligent. They seemed far more popular than ARVIN in most of the hamlets we visited. Like most Americans in South Vietnam, they have a very marked preference for minority groups and in particular the Cambodians. Whenever we came to a hamlet or met a squad of Popular Force troops, Major Digh would single out some dusky, smiling face and shout: 'Hi, *Kampot*!' *Kampot* is Vietnamese for Cambodian. The Negro sergeant got on particularly well with dark-skinned *Kampots* but all the Americans praised their fighting spirit and loyalty just as other Americans elsewhere in Vietnam praise the Montagnards, Nungs and Laotians or the minor religious sects such as the Hoa Hao and the Cao Dai. Few Americans praise the fighting spirit and loyalty of the ordinary Vietnamese. Yet the Vietcong also are ordinary Vietnamese.

The Americans took me on several trips along the canals that branch out from Co Do. To the north it was Hoa Hao territory and we did not need an escort because the Hoa Hao are solidly anti-Communist. Towards the south we soon came to the edge of contested territory where many peasants were thought to be V.C. supporters. We visited one of the outlying blockposts that had been overrun a few weeks ago with the loss of half of its men and I thought of Graham Greene's sad anecdote of the men on the watch tower. Had things changed much since Greene was here in the early 1950s? Even in 1963 the government still held the fort to the south which now lay in contested territory. In 1967, the major said, they hoped to win that fort back.

The present outpost is manned by the Popular Force auxiliaries who are often Hoa Hao or Cambodians. They seemed cheerful enough in spite of the recent disaster; and they joked about how one of their sampans had been overturned by a water buffalo. They peered with interest at a new grenade launcher and watched with amusement as various Vietnamese and American officers took pot shots at the larks on the barbed-wire fence on the other side of the ditch. Two of the bullets grazed a lark and sent a few feathers flying but none of the birds was squarely hit. After each shot they would flutter into the air and settle again on the same stretch of barbed wire a few yards further on. They sang throughout the bombardment. It occurred to me that I had seldom seen any large birds in this Vietnamese part of the Delta. Over the border in Cambodia I have seen hundreds of herons and egrets. In Vietnam there are only the larks and other small fowl. Geese and wild duck sometimes move high overhead but probably they are bound for the peaceful fields of Thailand, Cambodia and Laos. Birds detest the noise of bombs. They deserted the London parks in the blitz and many breeds disdained to come back until many years after the war. No doubt the same thing has happened in Vietnam.

Some of the Popular Force are secret V.C. supporters and many have friends or relatives with the guerillas. Sometimes they persuade these friends to desert the V.C. and exploit the government's *Chieu Hoi* ('open arms') programme that welcomes defectors back to the government side. One defector arrived while I was staying at Co Do and he was made welcome with coffee and cigarettes and compliments. The Americans asked him first of all if anyone else in his squad was willing to make the same choice and then, most important of all, what had prompted his own decision. His answer sounded honest. Perhaps two other men were ready to '*chieu hoi*' but most of the squad were staunch Vietcong. He had defected because of the constant air and artillery strikes; and because the V.C. had not paid him the money they promised. He did not seem to exaggerate and in fact his answers were sometimes counter to government propaganda. For example he said that the V.C. levied a fifteen per cent tax on the peasants within their territory although the government and Americans always claim that the tax is at least thirty per cent. Defectors who have spent several weeks in a *Chieu Hoi* centre soon learn to give the answers expected from them. They then talk of V.C. cruelty and oppression as their reasons for changing sides, when at first they were simply cowed by air and artillery strikes. The Americans asked this defector many questions about the V.C. leadership in the area because they 'wanted to find out if one of their leaders drinks too much or is messing around with somebody else's wife. Then we broadcast this over the V.C. territory. They all know it already, of course, but it impresses them to know that we know it too.' Never in history can an army have brought such weapons to bear on an enemy: bombs, howitzer shells, napalm, machine-gun and rifle bullets, grenades—and gossip about his sex-life.

There was plenty of gossip in Co Do as well, concerning the business practices of the Vietnamese officials. Nothing in Vietnam means quite what it says on the surface. For example, we went to a village one day to hear a debate about building a new bridge on the road to Can Tho. The village chief was behind the project and wanted the village people to pay fifty thousand piastres towards the cost. The Americans, too, supported the scheme because it would give the peasants 'a sense of sharing in local government.' But the villagers, when assembled in the schoolroom, raised many objections to paying. Last year had been a bad harvest. Why should they pay more money towards the bridge when they had already contributed taxes to the community chest? The interpreter confirmed what was quite clear from the mood of the meeting, that nobody but the village chief seemed really to want the bridge at all. The existing bridge was good enough for motor-cycles and small cars, while the peasants carried their crops to market by boat. The Americans and the Vietnamese replied that they needed a bridge because U.S.A.I.D. wanted to truck in cement for a new school. Moreover, U.S.A.I.D. believed that the villagers had to pay a tax to the Vietcong on anything taken by boat. They would not pay a tax if they sent their goods by truck. It seemed to me that, even for these reasons, the bridge was more valuable to the government than to the villagers. Later I learned from the villagers that they did indeed pay a tax on goods they took by sampan—but not a tax to the Vietcong. Instead they had to pay large sums of money to each of the three police check-points along the canal between Co Do and the Bassac river. Every trip by sampan was likely to cost about one pound. I have no doubt that certain people will benefit from the new bridge; but I think they will not be the villagers.

Yet, in spite of the war and the exploitation, most peasants live well. They have their rice and their ducks; their fish in the rainy season; their rats and snakes and snails in the dry. The tradesmen in Co Do have seldom enjoyed such affluence. One of the richest is Dong Van Na, who keeps a traditional medicine shop in a sampan moored near the Co Do bridge. He has acupuncture equipment, bottled snakes, a pickled monkey (for skin complaints), and a stuffed bear. His principal stock-in-trade is the cat which he keeps embalmed in a bottle of Best Foods Sandwich Spread. One scrape from the claws of this cat is said to drive out rheumatism; and, thanks to the widespread suffering from this malady, Mr Na has no need to work for more than a few hours a day. We squatted under the low roof of the boat while he showed us the various treasures: portraits of Lan Ong and Hoa Da, the gods of his special Buddhist sect, and a photograph of his own wife giving suck to a baby bear. He is very fond of animals and he keeps three dogs on the boat as well as his family and a large python. The latter was comatose after a meal of ten ducks. I asked Mr Na if his business had suffered because of the foreign doctors who now offered new cures and new medicines. No, he replied, his business had never been better, and as for these foreign doctors, he had not met them. 'I'm a simple man,' he said, 'and I've lived all my life in a sampan.'

One night the Americans showed a movie in their sitting-room, projecting the film on a muslin screen in the window. They and a few invited guests sat in easy chairs to enjoy the show. After a few minutes I started to notice signs of another audience. There were muffled laughs, cries of delight or fear and a constant mutter of comment and conversation. Then I realized that scores or even hundreds of village people had gathered outside in the courtyard to watch the obverse side of the film through the muslin screen. The American next to me smiled. 'They like cowboy movies best,' he said. 'They laugh and giggle at love scenes.'

They laughed and giggled a lot at the film we saw that night called *Women of the Prehistoric Planet*. It was a very bad but strangely disturbing movie with all sorts of implications for Vietnam. The space fleet of a very advanced galaxy was having trouble with some of its less advanced allies. The Santorians (I cannot vouch for the spelling) were proving especially difficult. Their dark skins and fragile Asian stature set them apart from the rest of the space crew who looked down on

Santorians as a backward, ungrateful people: 'You take everything from us and give nothing in return.' There is jealousy between the white and the Santorian women. Discontent and even mutiny break out in the space fleet. The action really begins when a space ship crashes upon a remote planet and a rescue party is sent to get the survivors. The whites are appalled by the savage jungle terrain of the new world. They meet landslides of papier-mache rocks, lizards enlarged to look like pterodactyls, and rivers of boiling mud that have to be crossed on a log. 'The air is so humid it's liquid,' one of the white men says. 'I imagine the Santorians could adapt to the climate very easily.' To us, on our side of the screen, this underdeveloped planet looked like Vietnam. To the Vietnamese on the other side of the screen, it must have been just nonsense. They cheered at the fights. They laughed at the slapstick scenes and the love scenes. And after the show was over, one of the audience lay as she had watched the performance, fast asleep in the courtyard.

*　　*　　*

Ever since going to Can Tho I had wanted to see Long Xuyen, which is the next town upstream on the Bassac but very different in character. For one thing, it is the stronghold of the Hoa Hao religious sect whose tempestuous and tragic history is one of the oddities of modern Vietnam. The founder of the sect, a young man named Huynh Phu So, heard the call to preach in 1939 after some sort of mystical ecstasy on his sick-bed. He travelled round the Delta proclaiming a revolutionary brand of Buddhism that soon became a private religion and then a political-military movement. The Hoa Hao first allied themselves with the Japanese. After the war they tried to co-operate with the Vietminh. The talks failed. The Vietminh massacred the Hoa Hao at Can Tho and the Hoa Hao massacred the Vietminh in the countryside. The French intervened against both sides who then united against the French until in 1947 the Vietminh executed the prophet Huynh Phu So. The Hoa Hao once again sided with the French until the French fell. Then they sided with Diem until Diem fell. Now they have sided with Ky who treats them with great favour. As a result, the Hoa Hao district round Long Xuyen is secure for the government and one of the parts of Vietnam where it is easy to get around and meet the people.

We were flown to Long Xuyen in a little four-seater aeroplane which deposited us on the air strip and flew straight on to Can Tho. The hut which served as an airport building was empty. There was no sign of a town in the flat plains round about. We walked to the main road and managed to hire a couple of cyclos whose drivers grinned and set off at full pedal. Five minutes later we came to a small village beside the Bassac where a ferry was waiting to take people across. The cyclo drivers urged us to cross on the ferry. We refused the offer and asked as many people as possible if this village was really Long Xuyen. At last the cyclo drivers admitted that it was not. They asked us to pay them off and transferred our bags to a larger and motor-powered cab. The machine sputtered to life, the crowds cheered and laughed and we set off back on the same road we had come. We drove for twenty minutes enjoying the hot sun and the breeze, and then the motor broke down. The bicycle cabs we had just overtaken overtook us; and the pretty girls waved and the old women cackled. The motor wheezed into action and brought us to Long Xuyen where it stopped dead. The beaming driver accepted the fare and then helped us to transfer our bags into another pair of pedalled cyclos. These went very well except uphill, so that we had to get out and walk when crossing a bridge.

I mention these trivia of our transport because they illustrate the good humour and cheerfulness of Long Xuyen. The Hoa Hao people are well-disposed towards foreigners and quite prepared to show it. Even the U.S.A.I.D. people, to whose offices we were taken, were not quite so soulful as others of their kind. They exchanged jokes with us and even jokes in Vietnamese with their staff. They were eager to show us some of their work and took us first by water taxi to see the hamlet of Vinh Chanh which lies on a tributary of the Bassac, nearly an hour away.

The water taxi is a slim wooden craft about thirty feet long and four feet wide in the centre. The bows are adorned with two garishly painted eyes, and there are five or six rows of seats for the passengers. Since villages in these parts are spread for many miles along the strips of land dividing the river from the paddy fields, water serves as the main means of transport. Villagers going to or from the town will hail one of these boats just as we hail a bus. 'They even hail our boat,' said the U.S. colonel who guided us, although I saw no signs of this on our journey. Perhaps the villagers did not like the sight of five white men and two sub-machine-guns.

These boat trips to and from Vinh Chanh were among the happiest times of my stay in Vietnam. The river was then near to high flood and almost covered the wooden piles of the houses on either bank. The children sat on their front porches and dangled their feet in the stream. The great pigs, in their sties propped over the river, looked as though they might soon be swept away to Can Tho. But these houses are not as frail as they might appear from the way they sway on their spindly props. The walls are of firm rush matting or sheets of pressed American beer cans; the supports may sway but the house sways with them in safety. The enormous water jars, which also have a religious meaning as guardians of the family spirits, stand on either side of the doorway that leads into the river.

The villagers smiled at us from the bank and the other water taxis shouted their greetings as we went by. Most of the other passengers were market women or serious older men in black but every now and then we would pass a boat full of twittering, laughing girls with their white *ao dais* trailing on either side in the breeze, their black conical hats tipped back on their heads, and their purple parasols twirling above them. These and the rich red-brown of the river, the soft green of the trees on the bank and the gentle putter of outboard motors completed the sense of fun and exhilaration.

The hamlet of Vinh Chanh had obviously not been notified of our arrival for the cadre commander looked very distressed to see us. The cadre members themselves were wearing the standard black pyjamas but many were bare-footed and several sported straw hats or green plastic trilbies. The important Vietnamese policeman who had come with us looked very displeased with their appearance. He became even more displeased when he walked into the main pagoda that serves the hamlet as public hall and found that most of the local policemen were lying about in their underwear enjoying a game of cards. The colonel assured us that none of the cadre were taking part in the game but my impressions were different.

The strip of land between the river and the rice paddies is only wide enough for a house, its garden and the path, so the village extends several miles down the river. In effect it is like a row of suburban villas in England, each with its garage and front and back gardens, extending along a road with some grand title like Wilberforce Avenue. These Vietnamese villagers, just like suburbanites, are anxious that each house in the row should display roughly the same degree of wealth and good taste. They were all built to the same height and breadth with the same shrine, like a bird-table, in front of the porch, the same big vases, the same kind of hand-carved furniture and the same Sony transistor radio.

Opponents of American intervention often proclaim that Vietnam is a poor country. If one measures wealth by industrial productivity this is indeed true. But large areas of South Vietnam, and in particular the Delta, are among the richest agricultural country in the world. The rice fields can support two fine crops every year. Every house is surrounded by pigs and geese so fat they can scarcely waddle; there is one farmer near Long Xuyen who has ten thousand geese that lay each day three thousand eggs that he can sell for threepence each. Most families also maintain a carp pool, boiling and bubbling with fish, at the back of the house. The fish are well fed because, quite apart from the worms and weeds that fall into the pond, the family erects a wooden privy over it and the carp and catfish feed on the excrement. The farmers told us that they move the fish to a clean-water pond at least a year before eating them but they did not reveal whether the same genteel rule applied to the fish they sell to the market.

If the soil is so rich, why does Communism still appeal to so many peasants? For one thing, the province around Long Xuyen is exceptionally fertile even for the Delta, and incomparably richer than the coastal lowlands of east and north Vietnam where the Communists have attracted most sympathy. But even around Long Xuyen the river people do not get their rightful share from the abundance of the river. We went with two American agricultural advisers to meet some more peasants near Long Xuyen. One of them, Phan Van Que, came up and said how grateful he was to the Americans for having shown him how to get a double crop of rice by the use of pumping. We admired the exceptionally tall and green paddy that grew on his land and then asked him about his earnings. He said, with evident honesty, that he and all his family had gone hungry last year but that this year he should break even. He explained that he paid between forty and fifty per cent of his earnings in rent every year to the landlady who owned about two hundred hectares in this neighbourhood. According to Vietnamese law, no one may own more than one hundred hectares. Since the defenders of the land system say that the Vietnamese enjoy a feudal society and need the beneficent rule of the mandarin families, I asked

Phan Van Que how often he saw his landlady. He replied: 'My family has lived here for four generations. I am sixty-five. I have never seen the lady who owns my land. But each year at the time of the rice harvest I see her cousins who come to collect the rent.' The Americans, I believe, have spent money well, in giving the peasants loans to buy fertilizers, insecticides, water pumps, tractors and seeds for experimental crops. Even the Vietcong have adopted some U.S.A.I.D. techniques, such as double-cropping. But even the Americans, congenital optimists, are dismayed by the dreadful anomalies of the social system in Vietnam. The rack-renting of peasants has flourished through every change of regime and in spite of all the advice against it. It will continue as long as the governments in Saigon are drawn from the class of the and lords themselves. The system is particularly wicked and wasteful because the landlords do not reinvest their rent in the soil. Only occasionally will they offer a peasant a loan at reasonable interest to make the land more productive. They much prefer to invest in Swiss banks or in night-clubs and bars in Saigon. A pious Hoa Hao like Phan Van Que is presumably deaf to Communist propaganda. Many peasants, who see the wealth of their fields grabbed by the oligarchy, turn bitter and side with the Vietcong.

Because the people around Long Xuyen are friendly to foreigners and not afraid to speak their mind, one gets some insight into the thoughts of the Vietnamese, who are so often reserved and sullen. I was amazed by their courtesy and intelligence and refinement. Compared to these quite simple peasants, our own farmers appear rather boorish and dull. While we were talking to Phan Van Que, his neighbour Phan Van Lu approached and greeted us with the usual pressure of palm against palm. He wanted to ask the Americans if they would give him a loan against the purchase of a tractor which he would share with a syndicate of his friends. He had spent several weeks seeing how other farmers employed their tractors and he was satisfied that his syndicate could soon get a substantial return on its capital. He had examined the relative merits of buying a new or a second-hand tractor and he was certain that a new one would in the end be cheaper. The Americans were delighted to hear this example of self-help and initiative. 'This is just great. This is just the kind of thing we're trying to do,' said one of them, who was curiously dressed in a solar topee. They thought Phan Van Lu was a really swell guy and they were just sure that he'd get his loan for a tractor. They said that it all went to show what could be done in Vietnam if only the people had motivation. Their optimism seemed to feed on itself and to reach almost dangerous proportions. For instance, while we were taking tea at his house, Phan Van Lu introduced his daughter who had been partially deaf and dumb since childhood. Phan Van Lu said how sad this had made him and how much he wanted to find a doctor to make her better. The Americans said that they'd fix up the best specialist in Saigon the next week and, whether because of their cheerful tone or because the remark was embellished by the translator, Phan Van Lu understood that his daughter would then be cured. It was difficult to explain to him that any treatment would be long and hard and not necessarily successful.

Phan Van Lu is exceptionally fortunate because he owns part of the land he farms and can therefore keep most of his earnings. As a result he has been able to build and furnish a very fine house with all the traditional furniture. There were octagonal chairs with marble inlaid seats, a stag's skull on the wall, a wooden sculpture showing ducks and rabbits and other creatures, some scrolls, a collection of old Chinese books, some advertisements for ladies' medicine, and the story of Cinderella in strip-cartoon form, showing her scorned, flogged, rescued and finally crowned as queen. An altar stands on a balcony which in turn is inscribed with Chinese characters: 'This family will have happiness for a thousand years if they are kind to everybody.' I am sure that Phan Van Lu is kind to man and beast. His five dogs looked friendly and well fed and even his Chinese rats (like our guinea pigs) are kept as pets rather than livestock. Phan Van Lu told us that when he went to Saigon to inspect different types of tractor, 'I was very careful about my money. I always went everywhere on foot so as to save the fare for the cyclo and I always kept a hold on my pockets.' The thought of mild Phan Van Lu at large in the greedy hell of Saigon has stuck in my mind as an illustration of old, pastoral Vietnam compared with the Vietnam of war and westernization.

We stayed in Long Xuyen as guests of a medical team from St Vincent's Hospital, Melbourne. The Australians and New Zealanders provide teams to assist at various hospitals in South Vietnam and each stays for about three months. The five doctors and four nurses from Melbourne were not only kind hosts but extraordinarily interesting

about their work in Long Xuyen hospital. The physical problems they
face are formidable. Before they arrived, there was only one doctor at
the hospital, which serves a district of one and a half million people.
Moreover, this doctor could only come in for a few hours each day as
he needed to make up his pay by private practice. The scanty Vietnamese staff is likely to be completely changed every time a new
Province Chief comes to power. Although the United States gives a
quarter of all its foreign aid to South Vietnam, little of this money
reaches the hospitals under state control. At Long Xuyen the patients
often have to sleep two to a bed. They are short of such basic equipment
as scalpels, bandages and streptomycin. The Australians have to go to
the local pharmacist to buy things like anti-acid powder.

Before we went to the hospital, one of the young surgeons, Kevin
King, gave us a gruesome forecast of what we should see. He described
the dirt and the stench and the overcrowding and the gory conditions
of operating. Perhaps because of these dreadful warnings, I found the
hospital much less frightening than I expected and in some ways
rather more cheerful than an English hospital. Since there are no nurses
at night, the relatives come into the hospital to care for and feed the
patients. You see a mother lying beside her sick daughter, an elder
sister crouched at the foot of a small boy's bed; and sometimes you see
one of the parents actually sleeping in the bed while the sick child in
plaster lies on the floor. Mr King said: 'I once took a man who was
protesting to the operating theatre. It turned out he was the patient's
brother who had got on to the bed while the patient went to town to
have a meal before the operation.' Like the other Australians, he looked
on the system with mixed exasperation and sympathy. 'The relatives
fiddle with the intravenous tubes, pull out the drain tubes you've just
put in and change the dressings. But if patients didn't have their
relatives they'd just rot. After all, it's what they're doing in England
now—letting the parents come to stay in the hospital. Half the cost
of the National Health Service would be cut if they introduced the
Vietnamese system. It would cut out the nurses for a start.' I asked Mr
King if the relatives did not pester the duty doctor to come to a patient
during the night. But apparently, far from calling the doctor for trifles,
the relatives will not seek help until the patient is 'très fatigué' as the
Vietnamese say, or 'half dead' as the British say, or 'bloody crook' as
the Aussies say. On one occasion, Mr King recalled, 'they came and

told me a man was *très fatigué*. His arm had been fractured by gunshot. The suture had broken and he was slowly bleeding to death while his relatives stood around going 'tch-tch' as if it was some extraordinary natural phenomenon. However, they will call in the doctor for some quite trifling ailment that disturbs them. For example they were deeply upset when a man got a needle in his shoulder.

An American doctor came to Long Xuyen to inspect the hospital and according to these Australians 'he almost went into a state of catatonic shock. He thought we were a most frightful lot of bums, that we should pull the whole place down and put up a twenty-million-dollar show-place. But you've got to work *with* the Vietnamese.' An Australian in the outpatients' department said that the way he worked would get him failed in any medical exam: patients with T.B., gunshot wounds, stomach cancer or malignant tumours are all kept in the same room. The patients and the relatives wander about to inspect the new cases. Children laugh and play on the floor. Even when the relatives have been turned out during the morning ward-round they peer in through the windows with all the dazed intensity of television viewers. But the atmosphere is more cheerful and much less frightening than that of a British hospital. Moreover, the Vietnamese are very resistant to infection. 'All the infections are softies here,' as Mr King said; 'they fold at the knees at the touch of penicillin.'

One of the problems is getting the wounded and sick to come to the hospital at an early stage of illness. The peasants are scared anyway by a big town like Long Xuyen and they are often treated with rudeness by one of the guards at the hospital gate. I was shown a young man who had a bullet smash through one hip, pass through the bladder and out through the other hip. He had waited six months until he could no longer walk before going to hospital. 'They'll come for miles in a cyclo with someone holding the patient in the back or they'll come in the bus with two gunshot wounds in the leg. They come in six or seven days after the onset of peritonitis. We operate in bare feet. I ruined a pair of Hush Puppies the first day because some of these abdomens are crammed with blood and pus. It's easier to clean feet than shoes.' If the sick are slow to enter the hospital, they are often even quicker to leave. They sometimes vanish after the operation and never appear again. The Australian medical team were still musing over the disappearance of two young men who were encased from the chest to the knees in plaster casts weighing ten stone each. Mr King said that they must have had eight relatives to carry them both off.

The Australian medical teams at Long Xuyen soon learn not to inquire too closely about the bullet, grenade and land-mine wounds of the patients. Some of the victims may be Vietcong who have changed out of their uniforms to get treatment at a civilian hospital. Others are hurt in private quarrels. One man, for instance, who suspected his wife of taking a lover, tossed a grenade at the house and wounded her mother and two sisters who now have adjoining beds at Long Xuyen hospital. The wife and her lover had not been at home at the time. However, most victims were wounded during attacks by one or other side in the war or by land-mines sown by both sides. I saw one small boy who had stepped on a mine and had been in plaster to the waist for the past two and a half months. He was still moaning and moving his head from side to side with the pain. The patients and relatives do not like to explain how, where or when the disasters happened. One mother brought in a four-year-old girl who had 'fallen and bumped her head.' The doctor examined the small nick in the child's forehead, dismissed it as fairly trivial, but allowed her to stay in the hospital overnight. The next day, just to make sure, the Australians X-rayed the child and discovered a .30-calibre bullet lodged in the left temporal lobe.

Amateur doctors in the villages favour cupping for all kinds of disease so that many patients arrive at the hospital with appalling blisters on their backs. They have an astounding resistance to pain and equally great stoicism. The surgeons in the casualty wards do incisions a foot long without giving the patient an anaesthetic. On a ward-round one morning we stopped by the bed of a small boy whose foot had been blown off by a grenade. He was clutching a pillow against his chest in an effort to keep from groaning with pain. 'Did you give him two Codeines this morning?' Mr King asked the Vietnamese male nurse. 'I gave him one last night,' said the nurse, who clearly thought this was more than enough for the case. 'Two, Mr Kiet,' the Australian said. 'Two Codeines every four hours.'

We followed the case of a man who had been blown up by a land-mine. At one stage in the treatment he was taken into the operating theatre where a Vietnamese surgeon prepared to amputate some of the fingers. The victim was given a local anaesthetic but, either because this

was ineffective or because of the pain in his other wounds, he wriggled about during the operation. There were several casual spectators in the theatre, who were interested that Gerald Scarfe should be drawing the event. One of them reproved the patient. 'Stay still! There's an artist here trying to draw you.' Although Scarfe asked the Vietnamese surgeon, for heaven's sake, not to let them disturb the poor man, the patient himself stiffened his body into a model's pose as the scissors severed his fingers.

*   *   *

Certain experts in Washington and Saigon have declared that the war in South Vietnam could soon be won if a physical fence of barbed wire and mines were built along the border with North Vietnam, Laos and Cambodia. The wags go even further. Everything would be dandy, they say, if only South Vietnam could be towed out to sea. Or would it? In fact, part of South Vietnam is already at sea—the island of Phu Quoc, lying thirty miles west of the mainland in the Gulf of Thailand, with a population of ten to twelve thousand living in a dagger-shaped piece of land measuring nineteen by eleven miles at the maximum length and breadth. Few foreign journalists visit Phu Quoc; it does not even appear on the map of South Vietnam which is given to visiting dignitaries by the American information machine in Saigon. Perhaps it is just as well. For this segregated patch of land, so helpfully 'towed out to sea' by nature, has all the problems known to the mainland and worse. Outside the four hamlets on the coast, Phu Quoc is entirely controlled by the Vietcong. Between seventy and ninety per cent of the islanders are Vietcong supporters. The Communists remain strong although they get no supplies or help from the mainland. These facts and estimates come from Americans on the island, one of whom said to me that 'the V.C. are very contented here. They eat better and live better than we do.'

The Air Vietnam planes land at Duong Dong on the west coast, the largest of the four villages on the island. The bay is filled with fishing junks and overlooked by a hideous marble statue of the Madonna that was foisted upon the Buddhist villagers by a devout Catholic District Chief. 'Very beautiful, sir,' said the U.S. Army interpreter, a Saigon man with a New York accent; 'here you can see red sails in the sunset

every night. But this town is no good, sir. They're eighty per cent
V.C.' We watched the fisherfolk gathered at evening under the old
Buddhist shrine on the cape, throwing hand grenades into the water
and scratching their names on the rocks. We drove through the little
town, which is two rows of houses on stilts, one on each bank of the
river, and we inspected the new camp by the airfield. 'That's the
whore-house, sir,' the interpreter said; 'just four girls for seven or eight
companies of troops.' He referred to some of the seven hundred
Vietnamese irregulars and territorials who support the American
Special Forces team on the island. It was rough out in the bay that
evening so that the Special Forces men had to water-ski down the river
and under the bridge and in among the sampans. The children thought
it was fun to splash in the water and watch the huge, blond men sweep
by at the end of the rope; but the old people glared and muttered. Even
in South Vietnam I have never felt so detested because of my size and
skin.

Phu Quoc is famous for fish sauce, dogs and pepper. The first is the
nuoc mam that makes every meal in Vietnam. It tastes good with rice
and meat but its smell is always repulsive, and in the factories almost
intolerable. They put anchovies into a great wooden vat and leave them
to rot and ferment; then the liquid is drawn off and pumped once more
into the vat. When this has been repeated three times, the *nuoc mam* is
poured into smaller tubs and left to mature. One manufacturer complained to me of the price of salt that had to come from the mainland,
and worse, the price of the vats which are eight feet high and bound
with a bamboo rope as thick as your thigh. And 'we have to use a pump
these days to pour the sauce back into the vats. There aren't enough
coolies to do the work.' The government and the Communists both
take a tax on fish sauce.

The Saigon Zoo has a special cage for the Phu Quoc dog and the zoo
director said that this breed was famous all over the world. It stands
about as high as a setter, has strong, bandy legs, and is generally sandy
coloured. The ridge of stiff hair on its spine runs back to front, which
makes the animal hard to stroke. The islanders do not eat dog although,
after a night of barking from four of them outside my room, I could
have found them a place on the menu. The island children lead the
puppies about on a string, which is a rare sight in Vietnam. They treat
the dogs well, which is even rarer. Even the Vietcong on Phu Quoc

keep dogs. 'Sometimes we try to creep up on them in the night,' said a U.S. officer, 'but we hear them banging their cow gongs as a signal. If they don't bang the gongs then the dogs start barking.'

Pepper, above all, has become a matter of politics. The plantations lie in the valleys inland, surrounded on two sides by the jungle hills. Since the Vietcong control the inland region they have no trouble in taking a tax on the pepper crop. Since pepper earns good money for little work, this tax is a prime source of revenue for the Communists in all south-western Vietnam. The Americans and their counterparts in the South Vietnamese administration have tried to prevent the Communists from collecting this tax by forcing the pepper planters to spend each night in Duong Dong. Anyone staying outside needs a permit which is valid for only four days. No planter can take out more than half a kilo of rice from the village in case he gives a share to the Vietcong. The logic of 'pacification' in Phu Quoc, just as in mainland South Vietnam, drives the people out of the countryside into the towns and villages. On the mainland they flee the terror of air strikes and artillery fire. On Phu Quoc they are frightened of being shot for moving about in V.C. territory. The American Special Forces team think that four thousand islanders, or a third of the total population, live outside the hamlets. They would like to see the proportion reduced. 'If people are around [in the countryside],' said one of the U.S. officers at Duong Dong, 'the V.C. have someone to tax, someone to give them food and someone to teach their bullshit to.'

The new Special Forces detachment (or Green Berets) arrived in Duong Dong last summer and now claim 'more kills than any A Team [of twelve men] in IV Corps area.' The Vietcong, so the Americans say, are quite content to 'be left alone and leave others alone ... If we never left the hamlets we'd never hear from them.' However, the Special Forces, backed by their Civilian Irregular Defence Group auxiliaries, have made frequent forays to the interior. They claim to have killed one hundred and ninety-two Vietcong since September. 'We don't take prisoners here,' said a Special Forces officer. 'If we did we'd interrogate them for two days, then the Vietnamese would give them a going-over for one day, and then they'd go to a rehabilitation centre for three months, and after that they'd go back to where they came from and next time they'd kill us.' The Special Forces men think that people join the Vietcong from fear of being called up in the Vietnamese army and because they want to stay on the pepper plantations rather than move to the hamlets. They freely admit that the villagers do not like the C.I.D.G. auxiliaries. The 'area assessment' of January 24th, 1967, which was given me by the Special Forces at Duong Dong, states clearly enough: 'The C.I.D.G. antagonize the people by rude, offensive behaviour. On occasion they have shot up the town of Duong Dong. The people regard the C.I.D.G. as only a step above an animal.' The C.I.D.G., like most of the mercenaries with the Special Forces, come from religious or racial minority groups. On Phu Quoc they are mostly of the Hoa Hao Buddhist sect, with a company of Nungs (a kind of peasant Chinese). The Special Forces believe there are Vietcong supporters among the C.I.D.G., and somebody in the camp tried to shoot the U.S. Commander. But they also have private and personal feuds which they settle by small-arms fire and grenades after drinking rum and rice wine in the bars of Duong Dong. One American called them 'Saigon cowboys' after the gangsters of the capital but most of the C.I.D.G. come from the country districts in the Delta. However, most of the worst 'Saigon cowboys' happen to be in Phu Quoc's small concentration camp, where they recently replaced the political prisoners. Their ringleader had escaped a few weeks ago and has joined the Vietcong. The District Chief, Captain Nguyen Nhu Vy, has offered a big reward for the bandit's recapture but he said that fighting the V.C. on this island was 'like trying to catch mice.' He was very proud, on the other hand, that he had managed to get ninety-eight per cent of the registered voters to go to the polls for the constitutional elections in September 1966. However, if eighty per cent of these were also V.C. supporters, the figure casts doubt on the claim that these polls were a triumph for Marshal Ky's government. My interview with the District Chief was cut short when the American Special Forces Major, who acts on the island in an advisory capacity, came into the the office and ordered me to leave so that the District Chief could talk to some senior U.S. officers. Their talk must have been serious, because when I rejoined the District Chief he complained anxiously about people who wanted to take his job just because he had made one mistake. He called for beer to give himself 'more motivation'.

The U.S. Army runs Phu Quoc except for the southernmost village of An Thoi, which is a naval base. Since the intervening land is controlled by the Vietcong, we had to journey there on a U.S. coastal control boat which kept a safe thousand metres away from the shore. An Thoi is also a fishing village, with *nuoc mam* factories and abundant dogs but, as so often in South Vietnam, it is worlds removed in character from its neighbour. All but a few of the two thousand three hundred villagers are Roman Catholics who came in a group from North Vietnam after the countries were divided. They are obviously anti-Communist, friendly towards the Americans and as cheerful in character as the Duong Dong villagers are morose. The neat houses and clean streets are unmistakeable evidence of their contentment. It was Sunday morning when we arrived and a naval officer took us to one of three celebrations of Mass at the local church. Burly American sailors, with sweat-stains spreading across the back of their shirts, knelt clumsily at prayer beside the Vietnamese. A few of them joined in the mournful, minor-key anthems. An officer read a lesson in English: 'Two hundred pennyworth of bread is not sufficient to them that everyone can take a loaf.' 'That's the parable of U.S.A.I.D.,' said the cynic kneeling on my right, but there was no doubting the piety of the service, in this hideous tin church with its reproductions of fourteen gory Victorian paintings of Christ's stumbling ascent to Calvary.

The nice old village chief Ngo Dinh Hoe plied us with beer after the service and said what an honour it was to talk French with a man from London. Before the war he had worked as an international radio operater in Hanoi. That was before 1946 when he started ten years of 'earthly hell' under Communist government. These villagers had been fishermen back in North Vietnam. They had chosen to come to Phu Quoc because there was empty land and fish in the sea and a beautiful climate that never got cold. 'When we came here there was nothing but trees and snakes,' he said, 'but the villagers are very hard-working and tough. Now we have rice fields and orchards—this red earth is very good. If only we could get rid of the Vietcong it would be just like heaven—just like a dream of women ... I'm very grateful for the help given us by the United States.'

The Navy argues, convincingly, that the Army has given too high an estimate of the V.C. support on the island. If there are two thousand anti-Communists in An Thoi alone, the rest of the island must be totally V.C. to provide an eighty per cent figure. And this is clearly not true. Why then should the Special Forces at Duong Dong wish to exaggerate the hostility? It could be that if every islander is an enemy, there are grounds for taking harsh measures of pacification. The Navy officers at An Thoi make just this accusation against the Special Forces. 'They are licensed killers,' said one indignant officer who has spent more than six months on the island. 'It's gun law. They shoot at everything that moves outside the four hamlets. But there are only a few V.C. on the island. I've been shot at more in——[here he named his home city in the United States]. None of them speaks Vietnamese. They call the Vietnamese 'slopes' and 'slant eyes' but I really like the Vietnamese and I know that one Vietnamese is worth ten of those ass-holes. More than half the V.C. they claim to have killed were farmers. One of them [he named one of the Special Forces team] tells how an old man in a blue shirt knelt down in front of him holding his hands together in the Vietnamese fashion—and he put five bullets through his head. The old man had no weapon. There was nothing wrong with his papers. He just didn't like the look of him ... They have a joke that their idea of *Chieu Hoi* is a mortar. They know that if they take a prisoner and the Vietnamese clear him he'll return, so they kill them first. They want to show they're real hard ... Look at the way they go water-skiing through the village, setting up a wake and frightening old women in their sampans ... When these monkeys clear a hamlet they burn down the houses and then make the villagers walk home. They don't do anything for them. They want to do it the hard way. If that's the war I don't want any part of it.'

One little detail of Phu Quoc life shows the difference in attitude of the U.S. Army and Navy there; indeed it is almost a parable of the war in South Vietnam. I noticed that many ratings aboard the Vietnamese navy junks had the words *Sat Cong* tattooed on their chests. I asked a Special Forces man what it meant. He explained that the slogan meant 'Kill the Communists,' and he said that the sailors got the tattoo as proof of their will to fight. He added that nobody with these words on his chest would be spared if taken prisoner by the Vietcong who 'would slit his throat.' A Navy officer gave me a quite different story.

'The junkies [the men in the Junk Force] all get that *Sat Cong* tattoo because there were many who didn't want to go into the forces. They didn't like the sea. So the Vietnamese navy tattooed them so that they couldn't get caught. But all that happens is that if the Vietcong catch them they tattoo an extra *Hoa* on the end and then let them go. *Sat Cong Hoa* means "Kill the Republic of Vietnam".'

The Vietcong on the island are probably neither as powerful nor as terrible as the Special Forces believe. The ideological differences are neither as fierce nor as clear as they seem from Washington and Peking. Most of the islanders, just like most of the mainland Vietnamese, do not want to be pushed around by either side. The majority do not respect the Saigon government; they do not want to be badgered by U.S. bombing and pacification. An important minority, including the Catholic refugees, have good reason to fear and distrust the Communists. Little Phu Quoc—that portion of Vietnam cut off from the neighbouring countries and towed out to sea—provides no remedy for the mainland problems. And that explains why it does not merit a halt in the brief inspection tours of American senators.

THE MOST LIKEABLE CAFÉ PEDLAR IN SAIGON SELLS OLD BOOKS AT double their real value. He is a small man with a pleasant smile and he speaks quite good French. Most of his books, too, are in French but if there is no sale he will offer you a collection of essays in English by General Giap, the North Vietnamese Communist general, and Henry Miller's *Tropic of Capricorn*. 'Tous les deux interdits,' he mutters. He also sells dirty pictures but only to the Americans. These pictures, just like his patter, are French.

I bought a book from him called *Stories and Legends of Indo-China* by Maurice Percheron. It is a 1955 edition but clearly the introduction by Percheron was written some years before the French left:

> At a distance of twenty-six days by steamboat or seven and a half days by aeroplane, there lives and prospers the most beautiful jewel of overseas France: Indo-China. It is the 'second France' as those Annamites say who have known how to appreciate our efforts. The traveller cannot hide his amazement at discovering big modern towns, wide roads with thousands of cars and buses, canals, fields purring with tractors, railways, aeroplanes threading the sky, and Pasteur Institutes.

There is just a hint in M. Percheron's imperial prose that not everyone was content in this other France. 'We have placed ourselves beside the natives,' he writes, 'and in spite of what is said by certain ingrates, full of presumption, we have given them our treasures beyond count.'

Today there are only three thousand French left in all Vietnam, compared with more than three hundred thousand Americans. Those French who remain live in fear of expropriation, expulsion and even imprisonment. Ever since General de Gaulle began his diplomatic efforts for neutralism in Indo-China, the government of South Vietnam has been trying to drive the last French out of the country. Diplomatic relations were severed in 1965. All imports from France had been stopped the previous year. Marshal Ky, who refers to de Gaulle in four-letter language, learned to fly jet planes in Algeria where he acquired an admiration for General Salan, the *pied noir* and traitor. Indeed, Ky has brought in French Algerian officers of violent right-wing views to advise him on how to defeat the Vietcong.

I met many Frenchmen in Saigon and other parts of the country and found them interesting out of all proportion to their numbers. Vietnam must be the only country in the world where the former colonial power has become identified with the extreme revolutionary element of the country it once ruled. This extraordinary about-turn has produced all kinds of psychological problems which are intriguing and even amusing. Besides, the French were constantly in the news. In September 1966, Ky's police arrested two prominent businessmen in Saigon who were accused of giving support to the Vietcong. Of course many French businessmen, just like their Chinese and Vietnamese colleagues, pay tax as protection money to the insurgents. Indeed, the American construction companies, oil companies and merchants pay the Vietcong not to molest their trucking operations. However, it suits the South Vietnamese government to make a special example of Frenchmen. This not only revives old prejudice against the French as colonialists but expresses Ky's loathing of 'neutralism'. A series of South Vietnamese governments have promised land reform in the Mekong Delta but what little land has been distributed to the peasants has been mostly French- rather than Vietnamese-owned. The French, as external landowners and capitalists, are easy scapegoats for the behaviour of South Vietnam's own greedy, incompetent ruling class. The government has also, for purely military reasons, taken over many French-owned rubber plantations that had been havens for Vietcong units. American defoliation air attacks have still further damaged those rubber estates where work continues. A French rubber planter (like almost all his compatriots in the country, he asked me not to use his name) said the Americans had caused far more harm to the rubber estate than had the Vietcong. 'The trees have been badly damaged by American spraying. The men of the forest [his term for the Vietcong] have not chopped the trees. They prefer to stand back and point to the damage done by the Americans.' This planter says that the men of the forest have total control in his area. They come to his house each

MARKET SCENE

evening to see if he has any visitors. 'They know everything that goes on. It's like the Vietnamese saying that everyone knows which side you sleep on at night. Once I was stopped by one of their road blocks on the way to Saigon. Now normally they won't let you carry on until they themselves have dispersed—just in case you warn the military. But I told them I had a plane to catch to go to France and they said: "Okay, we know you, you can go".' Many French planters and traders have similar easy relationships with the Vietcong, whom they often respect more than they do the government.

The French are losing their former hold on Vietnamese education and culture. The French government pays for four hundred and fifty teachers at primary and secondary school level, of whom about a hundred are Vietnamese citizens. It also provides about twenty teachers at lycées and universities, and fifty or so experts in agriculture, local government and medicine. The French Cultural Attaché, Claude Lafond, thought that about thirty thousand children in South Vietnam were now taught French, with Vietnamese as a second language. This was almost exactly the same as the number now taught English. But Vietnamese students are no longer allowed to visit France and must, if they want to study in French abroad, go to Belgium, Switzerland or Canada.

All these things explain the rather woebegone look of Frenchmen and French institutions in South Vietnam. They talk a great deal about the past when 'Hanoi was really *mignon*. There were no straw huts but nice little villas everywhere. Do you know Macon or Villefranche-sur-Saône? It was rather like that.' They complain that they have to work too hard to keep up their European standards. 'English life in the tropics was fun. Up at eight, start work at ten, tea at lunch and then *beaucoup de* sundowners. But for us it's hard work—ten to fifteen hours a day. That's why we look ten years older than we are.'

However, the French influence stays in Vietnam and will, I should guess, remain for decades after the Americans have been forgotten. This is not just because of a superficial Frenchness—the café habit, the sentimental affection for Paris, the snobbery about French wine and food and philosophical fashions. All these can be found among Viet-namese intellectuals, just as most educated Vietnamese speak French. (Even those who speak English as well tend to express themselves better in French.) The Frenchness extends to the mass of the population.

123

The Vietnamese delicacy and grace are very reminiscent of France. Their romantic conception of love, expressed in haunting and melancholy music, is also very French. Anyone who has heard a Vietnamese woman singing a French song—say 'Feuilles Mortes'—and then an American song, will recognize just how naturally she performs the one and how awkwardly the other. The cultural affinity between the two countries was demonstrated again in 1966 when, for the first time, a Vietnamese committed suicide by jumping off the Eiffel Tower.

The French who remain in Vietnam are eager to point out this cultural affinity. They are even more eager to claim how much better they get on with the Vietnamese than do the Americans. The intensity of their hatred for the Americans came to me as a shock. Many Frenchmen in Vietnam cannot talk for five minutes without introducing this favourite theme; and probably they expressed their feelings more mildly to me, an Anglo-Saxon, than they would have done to a fellow Frenchman. Often these complaints are purely material; the arrival of the Americans has spoiled the old French standard of living. Sometimes they are aesthetic in tone. I quote a few complaints as jotted down after talks with various Frenchmen:

'Fifteen years ago Vietnam was a paradise. Saigon was the pearl of the Orient. But it's now completely ruined by the Americans. Before, when there were only four thousand of them, we got on very well. We were very good friends although, surprisingly, two of my best friends were black. But then too many came and they ruined everything ... For us, who live off the land, it's terrible. Prices have trebled. We don't get paid in dollars or francs so we don't get any benefit from the black market exchange rate. Chicken and pork are out of the question for me now. A cyclo ride costs fifty piastres and a taxi is out of the question. Even the girls cost one thousand piastres for half an hour. We used to be able to have a good night out at a restaurant and then go across the river to the brothels. But now the drive alone is expensive and the girls all have a dose ... The Americans! They live off antibiotics and they drink water imported from the Philippines but they have still spread pox through Vietnam. And their food! You used to be able to eat superbly in Saigon. It was a real delight. But now it's steak sandwiches and ketchup, fish that comes in Cellophane from the United States, and as for their cheese! Do you know how I serve the American chicken? I cut it up, add oil, vinegar and mayonnaise, and serve it up as tunny fish ... The Americans! Three whites and one black round a table? That's not allowed over there. They're racists. In France, as you know, it doesn't matter whether you're black or yellow or green.'

A French diplomat expressed the same antagonism in an oblique but none the less deadly manner. He spoke in a quiet voice with considerable joy in his own cleverness. He began by pointing out that there were fewer Frenchmen in Vietnam than there were U.S. diplomats, A.I.D. men, not to mention C.I.A. men. Here he displayed a knowing smile. However, and here he lowered his voice until I could scarcely catch his words over the roar of the air-conditioning, the influence of the French was out of all importance to their numbers. This was partly because so many of them were professors and because the Vietnamese looked for their education to France. And then of course one had to remember the personal excellence of the French people who came here. The American civilians here (and he was not speaking about the troops who merely had their job to do) were not exactly suited to work overseas. Well, were they? He meant that they did not have any real inspiration—unlike the French who had come to Vietnam in search of a better life. An American doctor or expert, for instance, would think he was making a sacrifice if he gave up a month of his holidays to come to Vietnam; but a Frenchman would come over for four or five years. At this point the diplomat's voice became so soft and conspiratorial that in order to hear what he said I had almost to place my head against his. He wanted to make clear that this was simply his own private opinion but he believed that the Vietnamese would soon have to think again on the whole question of being a colony. They weren't really a nation. They hadn't been prepared for nationhood and they had suffered because the French had gone. It was the same thing in Africa, with the former British as well as the former French colonies. Abandoning them had been fine for Britain and France but was it really what these countries had wanted?

Most Frenchmen in Vietnam believe that America has expelled them in order to introduce her own colonial influence. 'They mucked us up in North Africa too,' said a middle-aged French businessman. 'Then they wanted to take over Indo-China. I know how they operate. I've read *The Men Who Rule The United States* and I know about the trusts— the copper and steel combines. It was economics that brought the Americans over here.' Men like this, who express the typical French view in Vietnam, are not left-wing in spite of their Marxist language. Most are on the right wing of politics but, in France, the right is traditionally anti-American and anti-big-business. The French say that the U.S. Air Force bombed the Michelin rubber plantations in Vietnam not to kill the Vietcong but to knock out competitors of American tyre companies. The French also accuse the C.I.A. of several murders of Frenchmen in South Vietnam—for which the Americans blame the Vietcong.

These Frenchmen, needless to say, are contemptuous of America's war effort. 'America now is in the same position that we were in twelve years ago—and they haven't even managed to keep the road open from Saigon to the north. If only we could have fought at Dien Bien Phu with all the equipment that the Americans have. Do you realize how many helicopters France had? Four! And the Americans now have two thousand!' The same speaker, who had himself fought with the French in Vietnam, said the Americans were 'fantastically naive. They don't realize that all these bar girls they go with pay a tax to the Vietcong and pass on information the Yanks give when they're drunk. And the cyclomen! They note where the Americans go and at what time. They scribble it all down. But the naive Americans ... ' And so the long-playing record moans on.

Many Americans reciprocate the loathing. 'The French are the Mafia here,' said a U.S. engineer. 'They control the gambling and the prostitution and opium. I hate them. The Vietnamese government is going to expropriate them all by next year. They're going to take everything those French bastards have got and I'm glad.' Earnest U.S.A.I.D. officials blame the French for having brought in the complicated and highly centralized system of local government. Ordinary troops blame the French for having brought the pox in the first place.

Fair-minded outsiders could say that the French are really responsible for most of the things that have gone wrong in Vietnam since the end of the Second World War. At no time between 1946 and 1954 did France come near to beating the rebels or bringing peace to the countryside. Cities like Saigon were far more dangerous in the early 'fifties than they are in the late 'sixties. Whatever the aims of 'U.S. monopoly capitalism', it has never behaved in quite such a ruthless way as the French rubber planters during colonial times, who conscripted slave labour to tap their trees. Americans may in private refer to the Vietnamese as 'slopes' (from slopehead) but the French referred to them publicly as *les jaunes*. The French today boast of their friendly relationship with the Vietnamese but during colonial times they never admitted them as members of any *cercle sportif*. Such arrogance would not be allowed to the U.S.A.I.D. advisers and Army officers—ever conscious of trying to create a good image. The few Americans whom I heard praising the French in Vietnam referred to their very brutality. 'No sir!' said a Californian Blimp, 'the French had the right idea. Bang 'em on the head, kick 'em in the ass. It's the only thing they understand.' Many Americans, maybe a majority, would agree with such a sentiment in private. Very few would dare to express it in public. That is a major difference between the colonial French and the muddled Americans.

To judge from the reports of people who visited Vietnam in the days of the French, the Vietnamese disliked them much more than they now dislike the Americans. Norman Lewis, who went there in the early 1950s, observed in *A Dragon Apparent* (incidentally the best book ever written about the country): 'As a European I had been invisible. My eyes never met those of a Vietnamese. There was no curious staring, no gesture or half-smile of recognition. I was ignored even by the children.' The Vietnamese today are still reserved and disinclined to talk about politics. But they are very polite to strangers. There is no sense of personal loathing except to those foreigners whose personal conduct has earned it. One can only envy Lewis his being ignored by the children.

The French were hated not as foreigners but as colonists. The South Vietnamese today, even those most opposed to American intervention, do not regard the Americans in the same way. Their hatred, if they are left-wing, is directed rather against the Vietnamese government. Perhaps the best comparison is with Eastern Europe twelve years ago. The many enemies of the regime were not hostile towards the Russians as people but rather towards their own Communist leaders who used the Russian troops for support. The French in Vietnam were hated because they claimed to rule by virtue of cultural and even racial superiority. The Americans do not make such claims.

The three thousand French who remain are incomparably better liked by the Vietnamese than are the five hundred thousand Americans.

For one thing, France wants an end to the war on the basis of neutralizing all Indo-China. This idea has wide support among ordinary Vietnamese although it is now illegal for them to advocate it. Moreover, the Vietnamese accept that most Frenchmen have long since abandoned their former imperial longings. The *pied noir* type, oddly enough, is just the kind of Frenchman to be approved of and employed by Marshal Ky. The Vietnamese intellectuals remain very fond of French culture and France. The Vietnamese colony in Paris has integrated successfully with the French. In fact, the Vietnamese regard France with just the same kind of affection that Indians feel for England. But it is France they like, not French rule.

A Frenchman runs the most enjoyable restaurant in Saigon. It is called 'Le Gaulois' and its menu boasts: 'No sweet music. No charming hostesses. No air-conditioning. No smart service. No decorations and sometimes no lights. BUT WHAT COOKING!' The few remaining French gather there to gossip, to drink Algerian wine and to play cards. One of them wears a beret. They are very well fed and have beautiful Vietnamese wives. On Bastille Day they become very drunk and patriotic. Like many Englishmen in Vietnam, I felt very drawn to the company of the French and inclined to forget their political wickedness. They behaved very badly in Vietnam but they behaved with characteristic style. After contemplating the stupendous, wasteful and largely useless American effort to reconstruct South Vietnam, it is tempting to sigh for the days of the French whose major technological innovations were contraptions for pressing a duck into soup and for filtering coffee.

Life gets harder each day for the few French remaining in Vietnam. Most are resigned to the prospect of having to go. 'But I won't go back to France,' one of them told me. 'I'm too old to start work again. I think I'll go to Africa. The young people don't want to go abroad any more, so it's still good for us older ones.' If the French do go, many Vietnamese will be sorry.

*   *   *

The most favoured hotels in Saigon are the ones where the Poles stay. These men are members of the International Control Commission for Indo-China and the only representatives of a Communist country who make official visits to South Vietnam. It is widely believed that the presence of Poles in a building ensures it against attack from the

Vietcong. They serve as a kind of a political lightning-conductor. For this reason many old Saigon visitors try to lodge at the Continental Hotel, where the I.C.C. has stayed for years. I had been at the Regal Hotel for more than a month before I discovered that here too there were Poles and that one actually lived in the room next to mine. I learned of it through the 'Fascist Potato', the plump, malevolent little American of extreme right-wing views. He had cornered me in the lobby one evening and lectured me for a while about how the United States should have bombed China years ago, how MacArthur was right and should have been made President. Then he mentioned that one of the Poles in the hotel had come up to him the other evening and started to try and make conversation. 'I told him "Poland Number Ten",' said the genial little fellow, 'and this seemed to get him rather burned up but, hell! the Poles are on the other side of the line from us.' I asked Mr Oscar to introduce me to some of the Poles and that evening I met the first of several. He was very depressed because of the rule that you could not bring girls into the hotel rooms but he cheered up when I told him about Cambodia where he was going on holiday. There, I said, the girls are sent to your room, whether you ask for them or not.

I next met the Poles a few days later. They all seemed to be called Stanislaw and they were all very excited because the supplies had just arrived from Hong Kong. One Stanislaw invited several of us upstairs to help drink the supplies which consisted of one crate of wine and another of vodka. We drank several bottles of wine and a bottle of whisky that Gerald Scarfe had brought from England. To judge from these Poles, the I.C.C. spent much of their time on drink for want of anything else to do. 'It's a complete farce, really,' Stanislaw said. 'Say we're stationed at one of the ports like Vung Tau. We go up to the airport in the morning and I say I have seen twelve warplanes coming in with American markings. The Canadian says he has seen six planes with no markings. Then we go back to the beach.' They travel to all parts of Indo-China but the situation they most dread is the De-Militarized Zone, which by that time was very far from demilitarized. One of these Stanislaws had been in a camp that was overrun by the Vietcong; he had had to inspect the bodies of Vietnamese policemen murdered by the Vietcong, and he had been both bombed and shelled by the Americans. In Hanoi, so he said, they spent most of their time getting drunk with the Russians and the French. Another good place to get drunk was the I.C.C. plane that runs from Hanoi to Vientiane (Laos), Pnom Penh (Cambodia) and then on to Saigon. Until the previous year, the Stanislaws said, this D.C.3. was equipped with an air hostess and a bar. After one of the planes was shot down over Laos the I.C.C. got rid of the hostess but kept the bar intact. One of the Stanislaws recalled how he boarded the plane at Hanoi after a very heavy evening of drinks with the Russians, and managed to get himself drunk again during the flesh-creeping journey across Laos where, apparently, all factions in the interminable civil war take pot-shots at this supposedly neutral plane.

The Poles, the Indians and the Canadians have an uneasy relationship on the I.C.C. At first the Indians and the Poles ganged up against the capitalistic Canadians. Since China attacked India, the Indians on the I.C.C. have ganged up with the Canadians against the Poles. But they are all one in disgust with their job in Indo-China. One senior Indian, according to the Stanislaws, became drunk on his first day and has not been sober since. A Canadian in Da Nang went out for an evening's drinking, blundered into the wrong house, and was savaged by dogs.

The Stanislaws were very, very Polish. One night we went to the Gaulois restaurant which they liked very much. They both liked the same waitress and seized hold of her hands from different ends of the table, pulling and uttering passionate invitations in Polish. They are pleasant company after the earnest Americans and, like most Poles, they are kept going by fantasy. One Stanislaw talks most of the time about Hungary and a village inn near Lake Balaton which he visits during the wine festival: 'There's some tourists, some Hungarian wenches in gypsy clothes and many barrels of wine. Just like operetta.' Later still he will start to talk about Barcelona: 'I went to a public house there. For example there was a room upstairs where I went with the girl. I have never seen a room like that. On one wall there was a red light and on the other a green light. And the bed was very big, as wide as it was long. For example you could perform on it any kinds of acrobatics. It was only a hundred pesetas for an hour—a long time, not a short time. So if, for example, you have strong loins you can do it two or three times. Spain is a beautiful country.'

*　　*　　*

The four hundred or so foreign journalists in Vietnam are so distinctive and sometimes so strange as to constitute a special minority of their own. Many are veterans of disaster in the Korean war, Algeria and points south, wearing the wrinkles and twitches of past disgust like the tags on their airline bags. A great many are old Congo hands. Many came straight here from the Congo with only a tour of Algeria in between. Conversation tends to revert, all too often, to which white Rhodesian mercenary kicked which Swede in the teeth in the bar of which night-club in Elisabethville. They have supped full of horror and of political incompetence. Like Joseph Conrad, who did his stints in both the Far East and the Congo, they know 'the fascination of the abomination.' They are sad and generally disillusioned. The excellent *New York Times* correspondent Jonathan Randall—late of the Congo, Algeria, Santa Domingo and now Vietnam—claims that he and Don Juan are the only men in all history who have been attacked by a statue: a monument of Lumumba, on being blown up by Tshombe's troops, hurled its stone beard at Randall's leg and caused him to cover the rest of the Congo crisis on crutches.

Vietnam, to the journalist, is not much more congenial than the Congo. The news-agency correspondents, the T.V. crews and, above all, the news photographers are obliged by their offices and their public to bring back the story of the war. Especially sad are the correspondents of local newspapers who have to produce a local angle. You can hear their plaintive queries after a battle: 'Were any of the K.I.A. from Pittsburg?'

Some reporters, however, profess to enjoy the fighting. Indeed one much wounded youngster replied to my question 'Why do you stay?' with 'It's the only war we've got and I just happen to like combat.' Most normal people do not. Those journalists who have to cover the military operations and spend most of their time with the troops have an uncomfortable and fairly dangerous job. When I went to arrange for transport to see a sporadic operation up in the north of the country, the military clerks regaled the reporters by discussing who had been 'zapped' or killed recently. 'How did the *Look* man get zapped?' 'He was unlucky. He just happened to be in the wrong place at the wrong time.' 'There was a little Malaysian newsman got zapped on his third day. That was just last week.' And so on. However, it is not always easy to find a battle, however hard one persists, and most reporters have been killed by land-mines or snipers' bullets in seemingly peaceful country or in plane crashes caused by risky flying in bad weather.

Some journalists become very military in manner and even appearance. One agency man I met impressed even the U.S. Marines with his craggy face and burnished equipment. His name and that of his news agency were blazoned across his chest, and the cross-straps over his broad shoulders supported an ammunition belt and a revolver whose handle was bound in green tape. On those few occasions when I wore uniform and went to a forward base in search of a battle, I found that my own appearance caused disappointment. For example I got off a transport plane at the forward air strip for Operation Hastings wearing gross U.S. fatigues purchased at too much speed on the Saigon black market. Mark Frankland of the *Observer* was wearing a tailored green uniform which he said was standard journalist wear but which looked like the walking-out clothes of a Vietcong colonel. The co-pilot, who had a Polish name, regarded us with appalled shock. 'Don't you carry guns?' he asked. 'No.' 'What country are you from?' 'Britain.' The pilot considered this information a moment, stared into the middle distance, then said in a conversational way: 'There's pressure on the pound, I hear.' Some of the journalists become very hearty. Their metal-plated boots crash on the floors of the Caravelle. They talk the execrable military jargon of 'K.I.A.' and 'clicks' and 'strikes'. They are loud and tough: 'This story's gonna intrigue the shit out of ya.' One comes to understand the importance of being Ernest Hemingway.

The journalist hero in *The Quiet American* points out that things are much worse for the soldier. 'With a return ticket, courage becomes an intellectual exercise, like a monk's flagellation. How much can I stick? Those poor devils [the Vietnamese soldiers] can't catch a plane home.' This realization produces a feeling of guilt in the serious, possibly neurotic, journalist. He feels obliged to prove himself under fire as expiation for his uncertainties about the moral rights of the war. Solemn, spectacled, middle-aged men, whose rightful habitat is the campus or the T.V. discussion room, can be found huddled under their ponchos in the jungle, recording for the benefit of their readers what it feels like to be under fire. They are sad and oh so serious. Some of the worst evenings I can recollect were spent in the company of American correspondents as they explained their views on rural reconstruction, the place of the hamlet in Vietnamese culture, the role of Marxism-Leninism in Vietcong thinking or the strategic goals of General Westmoreland. For some reasons I could not fathom, the problem of Vietnam becomes even more tedious when one is actually in the country. When *Time* and *Newsweek* arrived each week-end from the United States, I read them from cover to cover—except for the pages on Vietnam. It was a welcome change, after a few days spent with the U.S. press, to rejoin the more frivolous British journalists. Their conversation, at eight thousand miles remove, was the kind of wicked gossip one hears in El Vino's.

Senator Fulbright has criticized the United States Information Service because it has sometimes paid the air fare and expenses of foreign reporters wanting to go to South Vietnam. Even those journalists who go at their newspapers' expense are likely to be overwhelmed by the help and hospitality that they receive from the American propaganda machine. They get free flights on military planes and helicopters, free lodging in camp, and cheap shots of Scotch on the chlorinated rocks. The more distinguished columnists may be given the same treatment as visiting senators. They will be fitted out with a free uniform, entertained by a general and taken on an individual three-day fact-finding tour of the country. Journalists who receive such help are bound to be grateful. Moreover, they are likely to feel a natural sympathy for the pleasant and long-suffering G.I.s. In consequence there is a danger that they may become simply a part of the military propaganda machine. In *Doctor Zhivago*, Boris Pasternak caricatures the two types of war correspondent who covered the German front in the First World War. 'They collect gems of popular wisdom, they visit the wounded and construct new theories about the people's soul ... that's one type—and then there's the other—clipped speech, "sketches and scenes", scepticism and misanthropy ... ' Neither type, of course, could prophesy that the Tsar's army would turn on its own officers in revolt. The Americans in Vietnam seem to me equally far from reality. Even liberal journalists feel that criticism is a betrayal of the soldiers who take the real risks. They share Kipling's distaste for 'making mock of uniforms that guard you while you sleep'. Folksy or misanthropic, they find themselves sheltering under the USIS blanket.

The absurdity of 'communications' (their word) in South Vietnam is best displayed in the nightly briefings given at JUSPAO, the Joint

United States Public Affairs Organization. A series of officers representing different arms of the services come out one by one on to the dais like four carved evangelists on a medieval clock. Each reads out his news and answers questions. 'Could you clarify on the intensity of the strike on Thursday? Was it the hardest sortie-wise?' 'Yes, sortie-wise, I should say it was one of the hardest, Ted.' Markers on the wall-maps show the progress of Operation Paul Revere II or Operation Game Warden or Operation Masher. Sometimes these reports have an almost surrealist quality, like the announcement of an air strike on 'a Vietcong terrorist squad graduation ceremony.' 'Could you clarify as to the result of the body count the next day?' 'Negative to that one, Ted. A body count was impossible owing to the fact that the vicinity was under water.' 'Could you clarify if the Vietcong terrorist squad graduation ceremony was being held under water?'

There are plans for a special journalists' hotel in Saigon in which every room will have T.V. sets tuned to the U.S. 'media of communication'. It would be possible to learn the official figures of casualties or bomb damage without even venturing the two hundred yards to the JUSPAO building. But USIS, to do them justice, do not want journalists to stay in Saigon and reprint the official hand-outs. They encourage reporters to venture out into the country, to assist in military operations and even to risk their necks under fire. Unlike Kitchener, who dismissed the British war correspondents as 'drunken brutes', the American officers treat the press with friendship and frankness. It is more easy to speak to a U.S. general in battle than it is to get an interview with a British major in Aldershot. This friendliness will soon disappear if the correspondent's despatches annoy the officials of JUSPAO. Anyone with a 'negative publication pattern', to borrow the JUSPAO phrase, will be classified as a leftist and the fact will be made known to senior American personnel in the districts he visits. His sources of information will dry up; he will find himself shunned; and as likely as not he will go home to America.

Chapter Six THE HIGHLANDS

DARLAC PROVINCE LIES IN THE CENTRE OF SOUTH VIETNAM BUT, until fifteen years ago, few Vietnamese were allowed to settle here. The thinly peopled high plateau has always been the preserve of the 'Montagnards', as the French and now the Americans call them. The Vietnamese call them *Moi*, or savage, for the hill people are different in race and character from the Vietnamese. Anthropologists say that the Montagnards are the same stock as the Indonesians and Polynesians. They are dark and plump. They live in long-houses raised from the ground on poles. They are animists by religion and quite indifferent to money, politics, and education. Although they form less than ten per cent of the population of South Vietnam, the Montagnards have enjoyed a big influence because of their strength in the Central Highlands. The French encouraged them as a buffer between the Vietnamese and the Cambodians. They regarded them with the same kind of patronizing affection that the British showed towards Gurkhas and other hill tribesmen in India. The French used to contrast the loyal, humorous, childlike and above all *grateful* Montagnards with the proud, resentful, scheming and treacherous typewriter-wallahs of Saigon and Hanoi.

The Emperor Bao Dai, who had many hunting lodges throughout the Highlands, continued the French policy of excluding the Vietnamese. His successor Diem, however, brought in Catholic refugees from North Vietnam and set up strategic hamlets throughout the Highlands. He planned to create a composite highland people by mixing Montagnards in marriage with newcomers from Hué, his own birthplace, which he regarded as the intellectual capital of the country. He also tried to modernize the Montagnards and to prevent them from building houses on stilts. The result, in 1959, was the first of three Montagnard insurrections against the Saigon government. Although the Vietcong at first gained recruits from these dissidents, most Montagnards regarded all Vietnamese, whether Communist or conservative, with quite impartial loathing. The Americans who started to come as advisers during the late 1950s could not fail to exploit this discontent. The Montagnards, who remember only the good aspects of French rule, regarded the Americans as another kindly white race who would protect them against the greedy Vietnamese. The Special Forces teams quickly recruited loyal and bloodthirsty companies from the Montagnards. When the Montagnards' troops rose against the Vietnamese in 1964 and 1965 they did not harm their American officers. The outlaws who want an independent Montagnard state wage war against both the Vietcong and the government troops but they seldom touch the Americans. In fact, many Vietnamese claim that the shadowy rebel leadership is in league with equally shadowy agencies of the United States.

'If the Montagnards don't modernize,' said an American A.I.D. official, 'the same thing's going to happen to them that happened to the American Indian. They're going to be killed off or debased or locked up in a reservation.' He said this sadly, for he liked the Montagnard way of life. The Montagnard economy is especially old-fashioned. There is no shortage of tillable land but the tribesmen prefer to hunt or gather rosin in the forest. Most villages grow upland rice but at least half the crop goes to make rice wine. Those who work as labourers on the coffee and rubber plantations use their entire crop of rice for alcohol, which is taken by men, women and children and serves as religious offering, medicine, social enlivener, stimulant, sedative, aperitive and digestive, before, during and after all meals. If you go into any Montagnard village at any time of the day, at least half the inhabitants seem to be drunk. It has been said that if the Montagnards ever achieved their independent state, this new republic would have to be named Alcoholia. The French, when they ran the country, had to dragoon the Montagnards as forced labourers on the plantation. Even now, Montagnards are unwilling to take regular jobs except when they need cash for more alcohol or to buy extra animals for their innumerable sacrifices. Whenever a bad spirit threatens the village or home, the people will offer a chicken or a pig. In extreme cases they take a cow or a buffalo, tie it up to a tree, and slowly hack it to death with machetes. Each sacrifice has to be sealed with three or four days of total intoxication.

The Americans in the Highlands are anxious not to favour the

Montagnards against the Vietnamese. 'When the French left,' said a senior official in Banmethuot, capital of Darlac province, 'the Montagnards tended to look on the Special Forces as a surrogate. The Special Forces seemed to prefer them to the Vietnamese and vice versa. But in the last five months it's changed for the better. We've told the Montagnards they've got to settle their quarrel with the Vietnamese, because if they don't we're not going to help them.' The Americans profess to believe, though with off-the-record reservations, that the Saigon government is anxious to give the Montagnards a fair deal and to protect them against grasping Vietnamese officials and businessmen.

Meanwhile the U.S.A.I.D. mission, working with Special Forces teams, is trying to modernize the Montagnards by urging them into business. The A.I.D. mission in Banmethuot has started a Montagnard Handicraft Centre and Weaving Co-operative where the workers produce crossbows, baskets and carvings for sale to the tourist shops. The traditional carved monkeys and elephants are too rough for the market, so the Americans have brought examples of more saleable curios from the Philippines and Thailand. It is sad to compare the natural dignified Montagnard work with the sleek, book-end buffalo from Bangkok and the simpering, sexy, sub-Disney cat from Manila. The Montagnards have not yet learned to produce the statues of copulating elephants which are just now in vogue in the tourist boutiques of East Asia but they have had to change their style of art. One U.S.A.I.D. man, Mike Benge, reproved a carver for not giving enough chest to the statuette of a peasant woman and child: 'Not enough breast and shoulders. She looks like a gorilla.' In deference to the missionaries, the woodcarvers provide a miniature loin-cloth to cover the woman's hips but in accordance with their own tradition they have also carved very prominent genitals—under the cloth. The American in charge of the handicraft centre, Robert Myers, said that it was 'difficult to get the Montagnards oriented to a monetary economy. Their entrepreneurial sense is stunted. The Vietnamese take advantage of them in the towns because the Montagnards won't bargain. The idea of running a business is unheard of.'

It is hardly surprising that most of the good jobs go to Vietnamese. In Darlac, as in most of the highland provinces where the Montagnards are in the majority, the Province Chief and the District Chiefs are Vietnamese. Only Vietnamese is taught in the state schools, to the

137

great fury of most Montagnards. 'It's difficult for the children,' I was told by an old man in Buon Kram village, 'much more difficult than French. But they're made to learn it. The grown-ups only speak a few words of Vietnamese like "eat", "sleep", "right" and "left". It was peaceful here under the French. Now all these robbers have come. The Vietnamese came to the village and took ducks, pigs and rice. When we complained, the government said it was the Vietcong. But it wasn't; it was the government soldiers. But now it's better. The Vietnamese can't steal any more. Partly because the Americans are here and partly because we've got guns.'

Most Vietnamese with whom I have broached the subject dislike and despise the Montagnards. A liberal and enlightened girl recounted with mixed horror and mirth how she had met a Montagnard who actually thought she was educated because she spoke English and French and wore Western clothes. A Vietnamese official in Banmethuot, who entertained us to shrimp rolls, dried venison and whisky, explained in a confidential way that the Montagnards were quite savage. 'Do you know that at home they wear nothing more than a loin-cloth?' he said, making the clear comparison with his own neatly tailored suit and starched white shirt. 'They just don't bother to work except to eat and drink.' He despised the ceremonial uniforms of the Montagnards made of red cloth with embroidered lace. 'That's not traditional. That's just something they've all bought in the last few years.' The official's drawing-room was adorned with a model aeroplane from the 'twenties, a figure of Buddha from the 'thirties, and a 1940's nude statuette of the type that used to be popular in saloon bars. After the drinks and the talk about politics, his children lined up and sang 'Frère Jacques'.

All the Americans I have met in the Highlands prefer the Montagnards to the Vietnamese. An agricultural adviser who had been only a few weeks in Vietnam said: 'I'd much rather work with the Montagnards than with the Vietnamese. They listen to what you tell them and they don't steal and cheat as I believe the Vietnamese do.' He was trying to encourage the Montagnards to grow vegetables for the market and he had just arranged a sale to some U.S. Army Mess halls. He pointed out that 'the Montagnards don't use human manure on their vegetables like the Vietnamese do.' The Special Forces teams throughout the Highlands are proud of their Montagnard auxiliaries, or Civilian Irregular Defence Groups. At the same time they often distrust the *Loc Loung Doc Beit* (L.L.D.B.) who are their Vietnamese counterparts. 'I don't care what they tell you,' a Green Beret told me once in the Delta, 'but we say L.L.D.B. stands for "Lousy Little Dirty Bastard".' A Special Forces officer in the Highlands put the point rather more moderately: 'Sometimes I hate the Vietnamese. It's always "gimme! gimme!" I say if they want something they'll have to work for it. But in these *Buons* [the Montagnard villages] if you give the people some tin sheet or cement they'll build a school or a dispensary. They'll provide their own elephants to haul the timber.'

The Americans, who often suffer from 'culture shock' when obliged to mix with the Vietnamese, really enjoy the company of the primitive Montagnards. One American that I met insists that his drinking-water in Banmethuot should be boiled for fifteen minutes—but he freely drinks crude rice wine topped up with river-water. Those who turn away good Vietnamese roast pork, prawns and fish sauce will readily munch such Montagnard delicacies as grasshoppers and leopard meat. 'One day they offered us duck,' said a Special Forces sergeant, 'and it was really good, but I said to them how does a duck have such big bones? So they explained: "This very big duck. You know—whoof, whoof."' The Montagnard girls, although chaste, are stockier and more bosomy than the frail Vietnamese with their delicate child's bones. 'I have an adopted sister in one of the *buons*,' said a U.S.A.I.D. man, 'and when she wants me to have a drink of rice wine she simply picks me up and carries me across the long-house and sets me down beside her. I wake up at four o'clock in the morning and hear her thump-thumping the rice outside as though none of them ever had a hangover.' Most Americans in the Highlands wear one or more bracelets on their right wrists. These are the tokens that Montagnards give to a friend for whom they have offered a sacrifice. It is bad taste to be shocked by this blood-letting. 'They tie the cow up and beat it to death,' one Special Forces sergeant explained. 'It's brutal but it's kind of exciting.'

'Whenever we pay for sacrifices ... ' said a serious man from the C.I.A. I interrupted to ask when and why the U.S. Government pay for sacrifices. 'As Civic Action', he said, 'in promoting the unity of village life. But we say to them: "We respect your custom of sacrifice. But it's our custom not to torture animals." So we say to them that when they have a sacrifice it's not to last more than five minutes.'

Consideration to animals is not the only American influence on the Montagnards. In every village there is at least one shabby concrete house among the woven long-houses. The village chieftain, who knows by now that these modern houses are fashionable, will take all visitors to inspect the thick, hot walls and the garish tin roof. Some of the very modern Montagnards have abandoned their homes on stilts in favour of building at ground level although this is less comfortable and hygienic. Many Americans view these changes with sadness. For example Mr Benge, who has spent four years with the Montagnards, had a bitter note in his voice when he said that 'one of the signs of modernization is that the Montagnards used to drink rice wine out of buffalo horns and now they drink out of Army C ration cans.'

Even in distant villages one can see the recent influence of the Vietnamese and the Americans. At Buon Tri, about fifteen miles from the Cambodian border, I attended the burial of a small child in the cemetery in a forest clearing. The graves scattered around were ornamented with carved wooden egrets and elephants and the child's bier was spattered with sacrificial blood and buzzing with greedy flies. The food and drink which the family had provided to nourish the parting spirit of the child was contained in a case of Minute Maid orange juice, nine lacquered bowls, a gourd, a sauce bottle, and empty tins of River Queen mixed nuts and Players cocktail peanuts. The paid mourners were given coloured sarongs but the rest of the crowd wore bits of camouflage uniform, Vietnamese black pyjamas, blue jeans, red shorts and green berets. Most of the music came from traditional gongs—playing a fine eight-bar lament with shades of Beethoven—but some musicians banged out the tune on aluminium water pails or blew it out on a cheap mouth organ. Everyone—men, women and children, mourners and guests—was totally drunk; but although some were pleasantly drunk on rice wine, others were angry drunk on cheap rum bought in Banmethuot. The men tried out their few words of English: 'Sorry about that! No sweat! Red fink!'

Towards the end of the second day, the funeral party grew riotous. The different tribes, like the Mnong and the Rhade and the Laotians, started to quarrel among themselves and to exchange wild, drunken punches. A Mnong and a Laotian squared off to sing long ritual insults at one another. The boys and girls scooped up handfuls of rice-wine mash and soot to rub down each others' clothes. Only the children, as always with Montagnards, looked with serious stares at the pranks of their elders. As I came back to the village one of the Montagnard sentries leered and asked: 'Okay, sir! You neck Rhade girl?'

Festivities like this cause concern to the multitudinous Protestant missionaries from America. One Evangelical in Banmethuot has written in *Vietnam Today*, the magazine of the Christian and Missionary Alliance, 'WAR? YES! OPPORTUNITIES? MANY TIMES YES! In the very presence of destruction, waste and loss in conflict, the door to the tribesmen is opened wide. Shifted to and fro amidst the loud hammering of battle, he often comes to us when we cannot go to him. May the Church now be purified and strengthened to meet ALL her opportunities.' In non-Evangelical English, this means that the Montagnard refugees from the Vietcong, the South Vietnamese Army and the American bombing are coming under the influence of the missionaries. Another American missionary in Banmethuot, Robert Ziemer, said they now had between twelve and fifteen hundred baptized Christians among the Rhade alone. This was a great advance from the French days when there were few scriptures available in the Rhade tongue. When Mr Ziemer first came here in 1947 they had to make do with a few mimeographed Gospels according to St Mark. Since then he has translated the New Testament and the Psalms into Rhade, while a colleague has brought out most of the Old Testament except for a few books like Job and Kings. At first, he admitted, there was some difficulty in distinguishing between sacrifices of buffalo and the Sacrifice made by Christ. 'They paint a house with blood after building it. We have the Blood of the Lamb. But we teach them it's no longer necessary to have sacrifices because the Sacrifice has already been offered.' Also, he said, the Montagnards were once rather deficient in a sense of sin but this too had changed for the better. 'My predecessor said to me: "You will find that the people here will not weep over their sins." But I've lived to see it. Now they weep.' Thanks to Mr Ziemer and his friends, a large number of Montagnard women now wear black brassières, although many wear them round the base of the neck, thus leaving the breasts exposed.

I left Mr Ziemer's neat house, with its bundle of tracts and its harmonium, to visit Father Romeuf, a bushy bearded French Catholic priest who runs a missionary coffee plantation just the other side of

Banmethuot. As it was nearly noon he brought out the beer and the Pernod and offered us visitors 'something special, a glass of Algerian sacramental wine—they allow us a dozen bottles a year.' The Roman Catholics are stronger among the Vietnamese than among the Montagnards. Father Romeuf described a recent meeting of all the thirty priests in the area during which the Vietnamese passed a resolution asking pardon from the five French priests for having been unkind to them in the past and asking them to stay on in the country. The Church does not get on so well with the Americans. The Catholic missionary coffee plantation lies alongside the U.S. military airport in Banmethuot and one hears the loud-speaker instructions blaring over the noise of the helicopters. To the great fury of the French Catholics, the Americans last year decided to clear a strip of land round the air base by dropping defoliant chemicals along the perimeter. The poison used to clear a strip only fifteen yards wide was caught by the wind and wafted across the plantation. It killed many trees and left the coffee bushes covered with blackened leaves. It is a trivial incident when compared to much that happens in Vietnam, but it happened to Catholic French rather than Evangelical Americans; and in Vietnam such distinctions carry importance.

Americans often cite the Montagnards as one of their major 'success stories'. It is true that most Montagnards like the Americans and dislike the Vietcong. The guerrillas who operate in this area are largely North Vietnamese or Vietcong from another part of the country. Because there is little food for the Vietcong or cover from American aeroplanes, this whole central plateau is reasonably pacified. But the success story is rather misleading. The American popularity with the Montagnards depends on their reputation for standing up to the Vietnamese. It was easy to earn this reputation three years ago when all South Vietnam was in danger of going Communist and the Americans desperately needed friends. During this time they wooed not only the Montagnards but such Vietnamese minority groups as the Hoa Hao and Cao Dai religious sects. Now the United States wants to win and keep the confidence of the Vietnamese themselves and it is no longer expedient to befriend the minorities. If the Vietnamese government acts in a highhanded or unjust way to the Montagnards, the Americans will share some of the blame and the hatred.

*　　*　　*

The north-west corner of Darlac province has some of the only wild elephants left in South Vietnam. The Special Forces soldiers in Ban Don, where I stayed for five days, often hire them to carry supplies through the forests and turbulent streams and head-high bush. The team commander, Captain Robert Wolfe, said they were thinking of forming an elephant corps: 'For instance, if we got intelligence of V.C. at Buon Ya Soup about thirty kilometres away, it would take us a day and a half to get there on foot. But one elephant can get there in six to eight hours.' And a helicopter, one might have added, could get there in half an hour. Obviously it is no longer useful these days to ride into battle on elephant-back but the animals are excellent for transporting goods and at least a hundred times cheaper than helicopters.

The Special Forces closed their first camp at Ban Don in 1964 after the worst of the Montagnard rebellions. 'There weren't any elephants when we came back last August,' said Captain Wolfe. 'The Air Cavalry had been in shortly before and they'd knocked out three or four elephants. The villagers let the others go free. The Vietminh, the Vietcong and the Americans have all hit elephants.'

The North Vietnamese and the Vietcong both use elephants on the Ho Chi Minh trail into South Vietnam and this makes the animals a prime target for U.S. air strikes. The Special Forces Civic Action officer, Captain Jerry Walters, told us: 'The helicopter pilots have been shooting up the elephants and the jets have been dive-bombing them because they reckon that only the V.C. would use them. We've been trying to get the word back but I still carry an American flag and as soon as I hear a plane I put that on the back of the elephant.'

Captain Walters carried his Stars and Stripes on the elephant convoy which we joined from Ban Don to the village of Buon Brang Pak, about eight miles to the north. We had four cow elephants and their three young calves which the village chieftain said would have to go along with the mothers. Our cargo was rice, vegetable oil, blankets, and packets of children's toys. An Army doctor, Captain Lawrence Climo from New Haven, Connecticut, came along to treat the villagers. Interpreters and another Civic Action officer made up the convoy, The photographer Philip Jones-Griffiths and I, as newcomers were given the largest elephant.

Vietnamese elephants, unlike their Indian cousins, do not kneel to enable the rider to mount. You have to step on to the animal's head

THE AUTHOR ON AN ELEPHANT

from a suitable platform such as the top of a truck or a raised long-house. Provided she keeps her head still, you then balance yourself by placing a hand on the driver's shoulder, stepping on to the elephant's back and making yourself as comfortable as you can in the wooden basket.

The first twenty minutes on elephant-back are the worst. The motion, according to connoisseurs, is rougher but not quite so nauseating as a camel's and it is best to let your legs hang over the side of the basket. The elephant keeps up a moderate walking speed but will stop every few minutes to chew off a tasty shrub. The world is her restaurant and she will stop for snacks in spite of savage jabs from the goad of the driver. He steers her by pressing his feet on the base of her ears.

One soon encounters the minor hazards of elephant riding. Swarms of big red ants fall off the branches on to your hair and shirt. The elephant turns back her trunk to spray you with phlegm or dust. And as one U.S. sergeant remarked with uncharacteristic delicacy: 'It is not pleasant to be behind an elephant which is relieving itself of its extraneous gases.'

But after a time the elephant ride acquires its own rhythm and beauty. We forded a shallow stream in which the animals drank and showered and enjoyed themselves. We passed through a plain of tall, silken elephant grass which the Vietcong in these parts use as shelter for ambushes. The driver pointed out gaudy lizards and stick insects crouched on the tree trunks and branches. The American and Montagnard troops had lit many brush fires in this forest to rob the Vietcong of their shelter and once a gust of wind brought a ripple of flame to the convoy, the elephants reared on their hind legs, uttered a trumpeting squeal and bolted into the bamboo brush, but luckily none of the riders lost his balance.

After four hours of hard riding we reached the pretty village of Buon Brang Pak, about ten miles downstream from Ban Don. The local chief received us in his thatched long-house of cool woven bamboo and reed. The doctor inspected some sick children and dished out pills. Captain Walters gave out the blankets and food and then had the children line up for their bagfuls of sweets, towels, balloons (in the yellow and red of the Vietnamese flag) — and plastic toy elephants. The Civic Action team are fond of this village, which always responds well to suggestions of self-improvement.

'One time I gave them all bars of soap,' said Captain Walters, 'and when I went down to the river to bathe I could hardly get near the water. There were three or four hundred people wanting to try out their bars of soap. I wanted to get them towels too, so I wrote home to my church back home [in Coal Grove, Ohio] asking the minister if he could get the people to give us three hundred and fifty-four flowered towels for the women and a hundred and eighty striped towels for the men. I also asked him to get people to send pipes, because these Montagnards just love American pipes, even the corncobs. He wrote back to say he'd be sending the towels but he added a page and a half explaining why it was against his principles to send pipes because he was against smoking.'

The Montagnard men and women of Buon Brang Pak enjoy their hooch as much as their smoking. Like every village round about they insist that visitors drink several pints of home-made rice wine, which you suck through a long straw from a tall jar. We squatted round the jar and drank the required amount while the old men of the village topped up the brew with canfuls of river-water. The Americans who work in Montagnard country are used to drinking four or five pints of this brew on a day's tour of the villages: few will risk more than a pint before mounting an elephant.

The elephants' loads were lighter on the way home but the beasts were tired and so it was dark before we made camp. The forest was suddenly loud with bird cries on a cracked, falling scale. The smouldering pine trees burned like beacons in the night.

The elephants plodded on. Occasionally one would bang her trunk on the path with the noise of an axe hitting a hollow tree. The rumbling of their stomachs had the remote, subterranean sound of the London Underground when a train passes beneath your house. Another battalion of red ants dropped on my neck just as we came once more to the river crossing, but by this time we were all too tired to care about trifles. We were dusty and bruised and cramped as we jumped off the elephants on to army trucks and made for the shower and the mess tent. One of our party vowed he would never again get on an elephant, but the Special Forces troops make journeys like this three or four times a month. This form of transport is just as economical as practical. An elephant and her handler hire out at three or four dollars a day compared to as many hundred dollars to carry the cargo and personnel by helicopter. Moreover, as Captain Walters explained: 'We use elephants as much as possible because it stimulates the local economy.'

Years ago the Ban Don villagers used to live by training elephants and by selling them to zoos in Saigon and abroad. 'That's why they're so goddam lazy,' a Special Forces officer said. 'All they had to do was to catch elephants, sit on their butts and drink rice wine.'

The Montagnards use the grown elephants for collecting timber, transporting merchandise and hunting. Venison is part of their basic diet and they used to eat leopard and tiger. But the big cats have been almost wiped out because, as one village chief told me, 'there are too many guns around these days.' The Americans too go on these hunting expeditions at night. Sometimes they use a rifle with flashlight mounted to dazzle the game. Sometimes they kill with the traditional Montagnard crossbow which has the advantage of silence. In any case, as Captain Walters remarked, 'a day's hunting which would cost two or three hundred dollars at home, costs only six or seven here.'

Among the Montagnards, it is the women who own the property and therefore the elephants. The animal on which I rode belonged to a wealthy Laotian lady Mrs Kien, who hired it out to a driver named Mlar. 'My elephant likes the driver,' she said, 'but not me. I wouldn't dare go near it. It would hit me.' She normally gets a cut on the earnings made by the elephant although she allows Mr Mlar the total receipts from a major trip such as a convoy with the Americans.

The lady owners buy the elephants young for about a hundred dollars and pay for the long training which starts at the age of three. It is a brutal system of education. The driver ties the elephant to a tree and simply beats it into a state of submission. Meanwhile the owner offers a sacrifice for its good behaviour. 'If we want the elephant to be good,' said Mrs Kien, 'we sacrifice a cow or a buffalo—one buffalo for each elephant.' And a sacrificial buffalo costs from a hundred to a hundred and fifty dollars. In times of peace this would be a worthwhile investment for an elephant works about twenty years and may live to the age of a hundred. But few, these days, survive the bombs and machine-gun fire.

* * *

Dalat is so pleasant and so unlike the rest of South Vietnam that on several occasions during my stay I forgot for a moment or two where I

was and even in which continent. It is only one hundred and fifty miles
north-west of Saigon and only some fifty miles from entirely Vietcong
territory, but in mood and appearance it might be ten thousand miles
away. For one thing, the city lies at an altitude of four thousand five
hundred feet and the temperature stays for most of the time in the sixties.
The Vietcong have never been active in the surrounding province and
until last year there were few signs of the war. The people live off tourists
from Saigon and the sale of the excellent vegetables grown in this mild
climate. The Vietcong are content to exact a tax from every lorry of
produce sent by road from Dalat to Saigon and it is widely believed that
they use parts of the province as rest centres for Vietcong troops. There
are few Americans in and around Dalat. Their troops are unnecessary
because of the calm that prevails. Both the American civil and military
authorities try to discourage their people from going to Dalat on holiday
since this might create unpleasant disputes with the Vietnamese holiday-
makers. Few journalists and few T.V. teams ever visit Dalat, which is a
very tame place compared to the troubled districts of Vietnam. I found
it not only enjoyable but intriguing.

There was low cloud over Dalat as we came in to land and the first
view of the city was unattractive. There were damp, misty patches of
pine forest; grassland blotched with red mud, like a well used football
field; some peeling stucco palaces; and a hotel—it was soon to be our
hotel—the colour of gun-metal. The temperature at the airport was
twenty degrees colder than it had been at Saigon, and a light drizzle
played on our faces. The dripping pine trees, the stone walls, the chalets
with overhanging eaves, and the Lake of Sighs at the heart of the city,
all brought back memories of Europe. Some people compare Dalat to
the French-speaking part of Switzerland. It reminded me more of
Buxton in Derbyshire or even the Highlands of Scotland. A Vietnamese
poet in Greene's *The Quiet American* had gone to live at Dalat as the
nearest place in character to the Wordsworth country.

Dalat was once the favourite hill-station for French officials and
businessmen. The big hotel where we stayed retains its air of turn-of-the-
century grandeur. In Poona of Simla it would have been called the
Balmoral; the architecture suggests that the French too liked a Scottish,
pseudo-medieval style of architecture. The great central hall, panelled
in dark wood, is surrounded by galleries. The atmosphere of a hunting
lodge is still further induced by the antlers and horns on the wall, the

stuffed mongooses and foxes behind glass, and a number of wizened, indeterminate small animals. The taxidermist has tried to set their jaws in a snarl but given them only a goofy, buck-teethed grin. There is a glass-cased library of books, mostly novels from France between the wars, but including *Kim* and *King Solomon's Mines*. The young receptionist, as we came in, was trying to kill some of the big, slow flies on the counter. He would select a fly, aim at it with his spray gun and give a ferocious squirt. The flies seemed to be quite unharmed by the poison but they were blown on to the floor by the force of the wind.

The high season in Dalat lasts from November to May and this was the rainy month of September. There were only a few Vietnamese in the hotel and they were determined golfers. Each morning, regardless of rain, they appeared in vermilion golfing jackets, chattered and laughed a lot in the main hall, and banged their golf bags on the floor. There were also a few stray Americans, Japanese and English people who talked very softly, as people do in deserted hotels. The sun lounge was especially pleasant. The string band was silent during this off-season but the waiters would still bring tea and toast and you could lie back in a comfortable cane chair and stare out of the window on to the ornamental shrubs and the lake and the misty hills behind. Conversation was like hotel conversation in Buxton or Windermere: 'I think it's clearing up,' 'Yes, it looks a little brighter over there.' 'The major looked out of his window this morning and he thought it was clearing up ... ' 'They haven't given us much jam.' 'It was a good breakfast, wasn't it?' 'Yes, but the corner table had two eggs each with their bacon.' I thought of the generations of Frenchmen who must have sat in this sun lounge, digesting their too large lunch, listening in a state of torpid boredom to what their wives thought of the latest book from the library, dreaming of getting back to their Vietnamese girl-friends in Saigon or Hanoi.

Even inside the hotel I wore a jacket, a pullover, a shirt with long sleeves and a vest. The bedrooms were particularly cold but it was good to sleep under blankets again and leave the window open and never hear the whirr of a fan or feel the deathlike chill of the air conditioner. The mosquito nets were great white tents that covered the whole area of the bed.

The cool, highland parts of tropical lands have a curious quality of deception. One finds this in Kenya and Ethiopia, in Ecuador and

Bolivia. The climate and landscape suggest home; the vegetation and people belong to a strange world. And so it is in Dalat. Exotic tropical shrubs and banana trees are found among oaks and pines. Tigers, as well as deer, roam in this lake district. Because this is so like Derbyshire, I half expected to see parties of hikers from Manchester with rucksacks on their backs, and pale serious faces. Instead, one meets Vietnamese in plastic macintoshes or more exotic Montagnards in their tribal clothes. Even more curious to the Western eye are the Vietnamese who dress in the country style of three-piece tweed suit and tyrolean hat. I would stare at the little lake and the anglers and the bandstands where they play extracts from *Madam Butterfly* in the season, and then would try to visualize a map of the world and think to myself that Dalat was somewhere down in the bottom right-hand corner of Asia.

The straggling city itself is defaced by a gigantic, concrete, multi-level shopping centre of the kind that swindling property companies have foisted on English provincial cities. It has giant ramps and motorways but there are few cars to use them. Barefeet women tread the pretentious arcade and I was very glad to see that a couple of fortune-tellers had set up shop on the wide stairway between the street and the supermarket. Authentic Vietnam has reimposed its style on this foreign excrescence. The outside of the building is decked, indeed almost covered, with posters for Hynos, the toothpaste whose trademark is the face of a huge, grinning Negro. Since the Vietnamese, by tradition, think it good luck to have black teeth and a white face, I never understood why they would buy a paste whose effect, so the poster suggested, was to produce a black face and white teeth. The goods on display at the Dalat market were not the kind you normally see in such a shopping centre. I examined prodigious vegetables of the district, including Japanese radishes more than a foot long and slug-white. There were mounds of dried fish and crabs. I watched a young woman preparing a dead duck for display. She first arranged it into the most becoming position, then noticed that there was something wrong with the head. Elaborately and at great pains, she opened the duck's beak and tugged at the tongue to make it protrude in the correct, inviting way, as though the dead beast was blowing a raspberry.

Dalat has a lady mayor, Dr Nguyen Thi Hau, who is said to be one of the toughest right-wing politicians in Vietnam. The Americans in Dalat regard her with much favour and we persuaded them to take us along to her offices for an interview. She invited us to tea at five o'clock one evening. She is handsome, slight but strong in the face, and heavily made up, so that her eyes have a dark, lowering quality. She was wearing a black lace jacket, black pantaloons and a flowered orange *ao dai*. She was full of welcoming fluttering movements. She patted the sofa beside her to invite me to sit down; she giggled and clasped her hands together; she simpered girlishly at the compliments she received. She coyly reproached us all for our slowness in eating the tea of meat rolls, pâté, biscuits and cake.

Dr Hau comes from North Vietnam, where she trained to become a lawyer and where she was going to be a judge in 1953, before the Communists took power. Although she is now the only lady mayor in the country (here she simpered and squeezed her hands) she claims to have no ambition in politics. That may be so, but there is no denying her great political cunning. Even before our tea began we heard shouts from the street below and Dr Hau, affecting surprise, went out with us on to the balcony to look. 'Students!' she cried, and indicated a small and ragged bunch of young people. 'They are demonstrating for the elections.' In all South Vietnam at this time, the government was urging people to cast a vote for a constitutional assembly. Special cadres, such as this one at Dalat, were sent to the countryside to encourage people to register as a mark of confidence in the Ky regime. However, Dr Hau insisted: 'They are doing this all by themselves. We don't know anything about it. They are volunteers. They go to the hamlets and talk to people and play music and tell the people what the election is for and what the citizen of a free nation should do. They are very nice boys and girls but they are very independent.' I asked Dr Hau why students had taken part in the Buddhist riot a few months before in which seven people were killed. The smile disappeared from Dr Hau's face and she replied with great coldness: 'Out of the two thousand students in Dalat only five took part in the demonstration. Indeed the demonstrators kidnapped and beat some of the students because they had not joined in.'

Dr Hau twitted the U.S. advisers for not giving the city sufficient money. 'We have roads to repair, wells to drill, not enough electricity, not enough garbage trucks, no fire engine. We have to pay two point nine million piastres a year for the new market-place but'—and here she writhed and giggled—'it brings us four million a year in rent.' I asked her if she would welcome a U.S. Rest and Recreation Centre in

Dalat and her reply, with Americans listening, was a masterpiece of tact: 'I think it would be better to have an R. and R. camp on an island near Nha Trang. It would be a very nice trip on the ferry boat and the security would be total. And there would be no social problems for the city of Nha Trang.'

Dr Hau was very polite about England which she had visited on her way home from America. 'The rain in England makes the home more cosy. Our old songs, both classical and popular, take as one of their subjects the rain falling on the banana leaves and on the river. It is a very good romantic subject. I guess you have seen the Lake of Sighs. We call it that because when there is a wind the trees make a noise like the sound of sighs.' Here Dr Hau sat forward and started to sing in a low voice full of nasal twangs and swallowing glottal stops. The words were difficult to translate in their full beauty, she said, but roughly they meant: 'The raindrops falling on the banana leaves, drop by drop, mean the beginning of autumn.'

The brochure of the Dalat Tourist Office admits that hunting is 'temporarily suspended under the present situation.' One of its photographs shows a man with a hunting rifle who is squatting behind an enormous tiger, 'a record tiger killed in the High Plateau of Central Vietnam.' The name of the man and his face have been inked out so that he looks like a Negro. However, it is easy to read under the ink that the hunter was 'Mr Ngo-Dinh-Nhu, Political Adviser to the Government of Vietnam.' The former hunter was himself shot in 1963. His villa and Bao Dai's palace are now dusty museums of the Vietnamese aristocracy and even Dalat is no longer a safe resort for the rulers of Vietnam. The Vietcong had invaded the city the day before our arrival and had hoisted their flag over the cinema—and over the posters of Rock Hudson. They had shot the headmen of several neighbouring villages and they had massacred the ARVIN troops sent out against them.

At Dalat in the evenings we used to visit the floating café on the lake near the place where the pedalo fleet is moored. There we met a group of young Vietnamese on holiday. Two proved to be fighter pilots of VEENAF, the South Vietnamese Air Force. They were reckless scatterbrained types who used to beat up Dalat on their motor scooters. Their pretty girl-friends were obviously from a fast set; they were the only Vietnamese women I saw smoking. These young people lived for the day, because, as one of them said, they were not long for the world.

One of the pilots had trained in Texas, which he liked, but he had always felt homesick for Vietnam and he had sent back for some records of real Vietnamese music. 'All the songs were very sad,' he said, 'the Americans used to complain it was nothing but tears, tears, tears.'

'The raindrops falling on the banana leaves, drop by drop, mean the beginning of autumn.'

FOR A MONTH BEFOREHAND, EVERYBODY WAS LOOKING FORWARD to Tet, the lunar New Year, which fell in 1967 on February 8th. The old year had been the Year of the Horse according to Chinese astrological study, and this was to be the Year of the Goat. The goat, in Vietnam as in Europe, is reputed to be a randy creature, and its astrological number, thirty-five, is a synonym for virility. 'You *bamilam*— you thirty-five!' the bar girls say as they prod the ribs of a client; and the coming Year of the Goat was, as usual, the cause of some saucy articles in the newspapers. But even jokes about the Goat are made in a spirit of reverence, just as Catholics might make jokes about one of the saints who had human weaknesses, such as Doubting Thomas. Most Vietnamese I know are half-believers in astrological wonders. One girl, who speaks excellent English and French and is thoroughly Western in education, told me that marriage should not take place between people of the wrong years. Such a marriage might last for a few years but could not last for more than ten. Her family would never permit a marriage between the Years of the Bull and the Lion. The Mouse and the Lion, however, would make an ideal match. Many Vietnamese expected the Year of the Goat to bring some change in the country's politics. Those who wanted to step up the war reminded themselves that goat can also mean ram, which in turn can mean battering ram. The neutralists and the pacifists saw the goat as a symbol of love-making and pleasure and therefore of peace.

Before the war, according to old-timers, the celebrations for Tet went on for six or eight weeks and even this year they lasted for much more than the four-day truce agreed upon by the warring forces. The noise of fireworks started soon after Christmas and grew in violence over the weeks. There were rumours that Prime Minister Ky wanted to ban fireworks—as Diem had once done—but instead he gave them his special approval. Indeed several people said that this was the noisiest Tet in memory. 'They're a different kind of firework this year,' one friend assured me; 'they're using army gunpowder in the crackers, and the bangs aren't fun any more. They're a different kind of bang. Did you see that banner across one of the streets down town? A really brave man must have put it up. It says: "Haven't the country people of Vietnam suffered enough from explosions for twenty years without having to hear any more?" But Ky has encouraged the fireworks.'

The Chinese justify fireworks as a means of scaring away the evil spirits. The Vietnamese also believe that the bangs attract good spirits. All the merchants compete with each other for who can produce the most noise and therefore get most trade in the coming year; the shop down the road, selling china elephants, let off a thirty-foot string of fireworks on three successive days, each one of which must have cost thirty pounds. A merchant in Cholon, the sister city, let off a giant, multi-tiered ladder of fireworks that was said to have lasted half an hour and cost more than four hundred pounds. After a volley like this, the paper wrappers lie on the streets like a shower of crimson blossom; the reek of cordite hangs in the humid atmosphere. ARVIN celebrate Tet by firing thousands of rounds of bullets into the air and it was said that two rival regiments near Saigon let off such an interminable fusilade that all air traffic into Saigon had to be stopped in case they shot down one of the planes. When the Vietcong, on the first day after the truce, launched a mortar attack in central Saigon, the neighbours mistook the firing for firecrackers.

Everyone was determined to have fun at Tet. The men got out their best white shirts and went to the barber even at three times the normal price. Even biscuits and chocolates, which are the normal Tet gifts, were selling at grossly inflated rates to those of us who had not bought them well in advance. Indeed, when some hooligans shot up the cake shop next door, many neighbours attributed this to the high price of éclairs.

For us at the Regal Hotel, Tet proved a dismal occasion. An English journalist, a good personal friend, was found dead in his room on the afternoon of New Year's Day. It was a hot, desolate afternoon shattered by fireworks. Some Americans in the bar next door had acquired a number of giant fireworks, big as a half-pint mug, which they let off one by one in the doorway. The merchants out in the street fired off long ladders of crackers so that for nearly half an hour we could not make ourself understood on the phone to the hospital and the police. When the ambulance at last arrived, more than two hours after we found the body, it was accompanied by five orderlies, four soldiers and twenty policemen who crowded into the dead man's room or stamped about in the dark corridor.

Death on New Year's Day is the worst possible luck for a private house or a shop. When a dying rat was found in our street, the merchants shooed it along into Tu Do rather than let it die outside their premises. But this superstition does not apply to hotels which are places of transient residence. The staff were upset at our friend's death only because they missed a genial and popular guest.

Mr Oscar reminded me that life, especially here in Vietnam, was not really much of a thing. And Dan the waiter deplored the fact that so pleasant a man had died while so many bad men were still living. This thought reminded him of a favourite proverb, very Vietnamese: 'In times past, fish used to eat ants. Now ants eat fish.'

We were not allowed to attend the cremation of the journalist as the only crematorium in the country lies in an area partly controlled by the Vietcong.

EPILOGUE

At the end of January this year, the Vietcong launched an assault on most of the towns in South Vietnam. The war came home to millions of Vietnamese who had known it only from hearsay or from the newspapers. Most of the places and some of the people described in this book have been casualties of the Tet offensive.

Hué, Dalat and Banmethuot—all charming cities—were seized by the Vietcong and afterwards battered by the Americans. My Tho and the island of Phu Quoc saw heavy fighting. Of all the places described, only Long Xuyen appears to have escaped tragedy.

In Saigon itself the Vietcong made their headquarters at the An Quang pagoda and the racecourse. Most of my Vietnamese friends live in districts that have been bombed and shelled by the Americans.

'The rain falls on the banana leaves ... '

The misery continues in this most lovely of all countries.

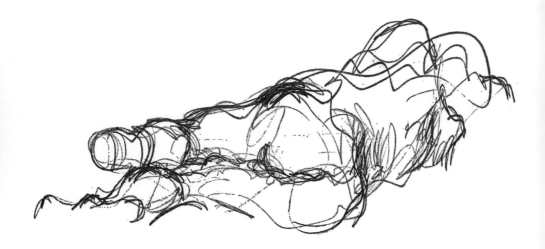

Elections in Saigon